The Secret Book of John

The Gnostic Gospel

Other books in the
SkyLight Illuminations Series

The Secret Book of John

The Gnostic Gospel

Annotated & Explained

Translation & Annotation
by Stevan Davies

Walking Together, Finding the Way
SKYLIGHT PATHS Publishing
Woodstock, Vermont

The Secret Book of John: The Gnostic Gospel
Annotated & Explained

2005 First Printing
Translation, annotation, and introductory material © 2005 by Stevan Davies

For information regarding permission to reprint material from this book, please mail or fax your request in writing to SkyLight Paths Publishing, Permissions Department, at the address / fax number listed below, or e-mail your request to permission@skylightpaths.com.

Library of Congress Cataloging-in-Publication Data
Davies, Stevan L., 1948–
The secret book of John : the Gnostic Gospel annotated & explained / translation & annotation by Stevan Davies.
p. cm.—(SkyLight illuminations series)
Includes bibliographical references.
ISBN 1-59473-082-2
1. Apocryphon of John—Commentaries. I. Apocryphon of John. English. 2005. II. Title. III. Series: SkyLight illuminations.
BT1392.A752D38 2005
229'.94—dc22
                                                                    2004024400

10 9 8 7 6 5 4 3 2 1
Manufactured in the United States of America
Cover Design: Walter C. Bumford III, Stockton, Massachusetts
Cover Art: Plate 3, *The First Book of Urizen* copy A, William Blake (1794). The Urizen poem is a narrative about the origins of the universe that closely parallels the Secret Book of John. In Blake's poem, the god Urizen separates himself from his fellow gods and creates self-consciousness. Urizen's fall into himself marks the creation of the universe and leads to his imprisonment in the material world.

SkyLight Paths Publishing is creating a place where people of different spiritual traditions come together for challenge and inspiration, a place where we can help each other understand the mystery that lies at the heart of our existence.

SkyLight Paths sees both believers and seekers as a community that increasingly transcends traditional boundaries of religion and denomination—people wanting to learn from each other, *walking together, finding the way.*

SkyLight Paths, "Walking Together, Finding the Way," and colophon are trademarks of LongHill Partners, Inc., registered in the U.S. Patent and Trademark Office.

Walking Together, Finding the Way
Published by SkyLight Paths Publishing
A Division of LongHill Partners, Inc.
Sunset Farm Offices, Route 4, P.O. Box 237
Woodstock, VT 05091
Tel: (802) 457-4000   Fax: (802) 457-4004
www.skylightpaths.com

Contents ☐

Preface □

Perhaps you are one of those remarkable people who experience an over-powering realization of the divinity of existence. You suddenly know that everything is divine and that within you lies an ocean of God. Will you know this all of the time and every day? No. You will crest and fall and submerge again into the mundane. The realization of divinity as the be-all and end-all, as the substance of your very self—that within which you live and move and have your being—does not dominate every day, although you wish it would. The ordinary world of aches and pains and approaching death, of trouble, temptation, sin, stress, and loss seems to rule almost all the time. And yet, sometimes you can seize what you seek and see glory everywhere and know yourself to be divine.

If you are one of those people, you are one with the Gnostics. You know what you truly are, that you are God, just as everyone else is. But, as a Gnostic, your existence in this ordinary and difficult world puzzles you. You ask, "How did I come to be here?" You don't seem to belong here. You belong in a world, a realm, of divinity. And it certainly seems that that divine realm is not everyday reality. But if, in full reality, every-thing that exists is God, why don't we always know this? Why do some people never even think it possible to be what, in their depths, they really are? Why don't we know who we are? How did we come to forget? What holds us back from perpetual realization of our divinity and what traps so many people into denying that their own divinity is even con-ceivable? These are the Gnostics' questions. The Secret Book of John is the Gnostics' answer.

Gnostics know that God is all and that they themselves are God. They experience this knowledge, this realization, and know that everyone else could share their experience. But they are continually thrown back into the seemingly hard material reality that tells them that they are merely flawed humans, kin to apes, doomed to die, ruled by a judgmental creator god who often does not show a fondness for people at all. Gnostics rebel against their churches and their priests, their Bible-based pastors whose obsession with God's supposed desire to control behavior seems not to be what true religion is about. To Gnostics, true religion, elite spirituality, is a realization of the divinity of every person, an experience of ascent to the divine homeland. It is a knowledge of the way we once were as God and of the processes by which God came to be so self-forgetful as to become us, mere human beings under the control of another lesser god. Those are the lessons taught in the Gnostic Gospel, the Secret Book of John.

Gnosticism is a religion of rebels: creative thinkers whose works were systematically destroyed by orthodox Christianity between the second and the sixth centuries CE. Gnostics were the "other" to the growth of orthodoxy; they lived in the home of heresy for they were the source of self-assertiveness against the episcopal demand for sameness. They persisted in the shadows, in certain Sufi sects, in the Christian Cathar movement, and perhaps even among the Knights Templar and the Rosicrucian orders. Only recently have the old Gnostics spoken aloud again. Their speech resounds in the documents of the Nag Hammadi Library buried seventeen hundred years ago in Upper Egypt, discovered again in 1945, and read today by spiritual seekers throughout the world. Their main document, their central myth, their theory of the origin and structure of reality is a text called the Secret Book of John. In this text we learn how God fell and became us and how, through knowing that story, we can return to glory and be absorbed again into God. This new annotated edition of the Secret Book of John will help you take up the challenge of reading the primary Gnostic myth. It discusses the principal themes of the Secret Book of John and explains the historical and spiritual contexts as they arise. The general reader and the spiritual seeker will come away from reading it with good insight into the fundamental ideas of the Gnostic religion.

Introduction

The Secret Book of John is the most significant and influential text of the ancient Gnostic religion. Written in Greek during the early second century CE by an unknown author, the Secret Book of John became the source of a host of other Gnostic texts, myths, and cosmic systems. In Greek its title is *Apocryphon Johannis* and it is known in scholarship as the *Apocryphon of John*. The word *apocryphon* means "secret" or "hidden." The Secret Book of John tells the story of the devolution of God from perfect Oneness to imprisonment in the material world. If you look at some of its sections it is Christian, in others it is a version of Platonic philosophy, frequently it is a book of Jewish commentary on Moses's Torah. It is all of these things in ways that the authorities of orthodoxy in Christianity, Platonism, and Judaism totally rejected. It is the foundation of something else, something supported by the historical tripod of Christianity, Platonism, and Judaism, but it is none of those. It is the expression of a whole new point of view, new in its own time, and new in our time, for the full version of the Secret Book of John was only discovered recently, although its existence was known long before.

Around 180 CE a bishop of Lyon, a man named Irenaeus, decided to write a book attacking all forms of Christianity he knew of that differed from the form of which he approved. All other forms were, in his mind, heresies and most fit into the very broad, ill-defined category of religion we call Gnosticism. His five-volume book, entitled *Against Heresies,* takes a violently negative view of its subjects. Fortunately, Irenaeus does describe in considerable detail what he despises. In chapter 29 of his first volume, Irenaeus outlines some sections of the Secret Book of John in detail. This tells us that the Secret Book of John must have been written well before 180 CE (although not in the exact form we have it now) and we know that its circulation included Gaul (today's France), in order for Irenaeus to have read it.

In Cairo in 1896, German scholar Carl Reinhardt bought an ancient book written in Coptic, the ancient Egyptian language written in mainly Greek letters. That book, which is now known as the Berlin Gnostic Codex, turned out to contain three important Gnostic writings: the Gospel of Mary, the Secret Book of John, and the Wisdom of Jesus Christ. Because of the two world wars, these texts were not made generally available until the 1950s. By that time an even more important discovery had been made.

In Nag Hammadi, Egypt, in 1945, local workers stumbled upon a very large jar in which were hidden thirteen books containing a total of fifty-two documents of ancient Gnostic wisdom. Some were very badly damaged, some were slightly damaged, and some remained in excellent condition. For the study of early Christianity in its unorthodox forms, and probably also in its orthodox form, this was the most important manuscript discovery ever made.

The document that appears most frequently in the Nag Hammadi collection is the Secret Book of John. Three copies were found there; no other text is found more than twice. In all three cases, the Secret Book of John is the first document bound into its volume. Book II of the Nag Hammadi Library begins with the Secret Book of John, which is then followed by the Gospel of Thomas, the Gospel of Philip, and four other texts. Book III begins with the Secret Book of John, followed by the Gospel of the Egyptians, earlier and later versions of the Wisdom of Jesus Christ, and finally, the Dialogue of the Savior. Book IV starts with the Secret Book of John, which is followed by the Gospel of the Egyptians. This prominent placement clearly shows that the Secret Book of John provided the context in which much of the Nag Hammadi Library was read. For example, people who read Book II read the Gospel of Thomas in light of what they had just completed, the Secret Book of John. By contrast, today most people who read and study the Gospel of Thomas do so with the canonical Gospels in mind.

Ancient books were sometimes bound in covers made from glued-together pieces of papyrus: trash pages from worn-out books, thrown-away letters, out-of-date commercial documents, and so forth. This material can be painstakingly separated and read, providing valuable historical context for the text enclosed. When the covers of the Nag Hammadi books were taken apart in this way, it turned out that the scraps of papyrus in them sometimes contained dates, the latest of which is 348 CE. Some of that papyrus seems to have originated in a Christian monastery. There were ancient monasteries in the vicinity of Nag Hammadi, and some scholars are convinced that the Gnostic library found hidden in 1945 was once part of an orthodox Christian monastic library. Others are skeptical, saying that the discarded papyrus used for book covers could just as well have come from a community trash heap where monks and others threw scraps of paper away. Be that as it may, we can be sure that most of the Nag Hammadi books were copied and bound in the middle of the fourth century CE; the Berlin Gnostic Codex comes from the same period.

We now have four copies of the Secret Book of John: three from Nag Hammadi, Egypt, and the fourth in the Berlin Gnostic Codex from an unknown place in Egypt. All are written in Coptic, but like the other Nag Hammadi documents, they were originally written in Greek, as evidenced by the many Greek words that remain untranslated in the Coptic manuscripts. Specialists have concluded that these four copies represent three different Coptic translations. They fall into two categories: a long version of the Secret Book of John (found in Nag Hammadi Books II and IV) and a shorter version (found in Nag Hammadi Book III and in the Berlin Gnostic Codex). The difference is, basically, that the long version contains two sections that do not appear in the short version: a detailed exposition of the creation of primordial Adam by many different demons, and a three-part poem about the Providence of God journeying into this world. Apart from these, the longer and shorter versions generally agree on main points while differing in details.

The Gnostic Gospel

The Secret Book of John is "The Gnostic Gospel" in the sense that Paul meant when he wrote of there being many gospels, although, of course, Paul believed only his own gospel came from God. Paul uses the word *gospel* to mean a message about the nature of God and Christ and Salvation not a narrative biography of Jesus, as we now often use the word. The Secret Book of John has no biographical narrative apart from its opening lines. Nevertheless, because it is a message about the nature of God and Christ and Salvation it is a "gospel," although certainly not one that Paul would have approved.

It is a "Gnostic" gospel because it teaches that salvation comes from knowledge, or "gnosis": knowledge of our divine nature, our divine origin, and our ultimate goal, which is to be restored to our rightful place within God. And it is "the" Gnostic Gospel because it has first place among Gnostic writings both literally (in three Nag Hammadi volumes) and figuratively. It gives the basic Gnostic message, one that other Gnostic texts, many of which are extensive and creative revisions of sections of the Secret Book of John, also give in their varied and creative ways.

The Secret Book of John begins with a brief narrative passage telling us that what we are reading is a revelation of the ascended Jesus Christ to his disciple John, son of Zebedee. The revelation itself occupies the text until the end, when Jesus and John appear once again to bring the book to its conclusion. Because of these beginning and concluding passages, the whole text presents itself as Christian: a revelation by Jesus to one of his disciples. However, these sections were added to a preexisting mythological book that was not Christian at all. It was mythologized Middle Platonism combined with a Jewish inversion of the Genesis story and a Gnostic theory of fall and salvation. Whether this non-Christian version of the Secret Book of John was chronologically pre-Christian is debatable; many scholars think it probably came into being toward the end of the first century CE, but it is possible that it was in writing, in one form or another, a century or more before that.

Because the Secret Book of John was so important to the Gnostics, over the centuries many scribes added clarifying comments to it. Because the Gnostics valued change and creativity, which the orthodox condemned as the matrix of heresy, the Secret Book of John went through many copies, versions, and editions. Accordingly, the copies we have today contain wide variations of comments and vocabulary blended into the main text. It does not flow smoothly, but when you get used to it, it's not so confusing.

The Secret Book of John tells the history of God, beginning with passages that stress God's incomprehensible nature. At first we hear that God, "the One," cannot be discussed in words, but as we move along in the myth, the One becomes increasingly comprehensible. Soon we hear that the Godhead apprehends itself in the surrounding supernal light and twoness emerges: God and God Aware of God or God and the self-consciousness of God.

As the myth continues, the self-consciousness of God asks for and receives a set of mental faculties that appear to be structured in the manner of mandalas, circular diagrams with four different quadrants surrounding a more important central element. These mental faculties are described as if they constitute the royal court of heaven. We are reading about the gradual emergence of God's mind, a set of interacting capacities that come into being below, as it were, the ultimate level of the Incomprehensible One. This is a developmental psychology, a descriptive Middle-Platonic philosophy, and most importantly, a cosmic mythology all rolled into one.

After the full development of the mind of God—a fullness called *pleroma* in Greek—has been outlined, a crisis occurs. One aspect of God's mind, its wisdom—*Sophia* in Greek—seeks to know an image of herself apart from the fullness. Sophia's individual effort has disastrous results.

She discovers an image that is not the full mind of God at all, but a monster named Yaldabaoth who appears to exist outside of God. This is a mistake on God's part (for God's wisdom is part of God at all times) and is perhaps even God going insane and imagining reality outside of God that cannot be. The consequences of this mistake occupy the rest of the Secret Book of John.

We hear that Yaldabaoth, the being brought into existence by Sophia, begins to construct a world based on his inadequate, half-witted knowledge of the higher realms of God's mind. This is an artificial world, a bad imitation of the real world, a world that becomes our world. Yaldabaoth brings beings into existence who are his subordinate rulers: demons who dominate this lower, artificial world. The divine powers of the wisdom of God, without whom nothing could exist, also act within this lower world.

To return Wisdom's stolen power to God, a plan comes down from the whole fullness of the mind of God. Yaldabaoth will be deceived so that he blows his power into a creature who will in turn restore that power to the higher realms. The divine realms are clearly revealed to Yaldabaoth and his demons, and they decide to construct a being modeled on that revelation. That being is Adam; he gains life and mobility only after Yaldabaoth's power is blown into him.

The higher realms of God send down mental power symbolized as Eve to assist Adam; both are, of course, symbolic beings and not real people. Yaldabaoth and his demons scheme to imprison Adam and Eve in matter in this world, but the higher realms send down revelation to assist them. The book concludes with a three-part hymn wherein revelation, called Providence, comes into the world to release us from bondage, for we all are Adam and Eve.

The Goal of Gnostic Salvation

This is a mythology. It is a story of how things came to be the way they are: a story that sets the pattern for everything forever, or as this myth has it, until forever is over. The ultimate goal of humanity is to come to understand this myth, the gospel of the Secret Book of John, in such a way that the pattern of devolution from the fullness of God to humanity's imprisonment in matter is reversed. To understand the events of our fall reveals to us a map for our journey of ascent. We will emerge free from matter, rise above Yaldabaoth and his demons, return to an established position in the mind of God, and never leave again. The mistake of Sophia will be resolved and wisdom will be fully restored to God. The mind of God will be fully sane and healed.

The Gnostic myth is a tale of the growth of God's mental disintegration. The myth reaches its most unhappy form when the Godhead has not only forgotten who God is but does not even know that God truly exists and begins to worship the artificial deity Yaldabaoth as creator of an external world. In the depths of God's fall, the Godhead believes itself to be human and worships Yaldabaoth as the god of the Hebrew Bible. Gnostic texts concern themselves with the attempt by God to return to a state of mental harmony, union, and completion of self-recognition. The Gnostic religion has at its core the view that the world as known by ordinary people is a symptom of God's self-forgetfulness. As a symptom it is evil, but it is so only as the aches of a self-deluded psychosomatically ill person are evil. Not only are the aches nonexistent, but there is a healthy body really there all the time. For Gnosticism, the external and material world is only apparently evil because, to the consciousness of the enlightened individual, the pleroma, or mind of God, is really there all the time.

There is no evil realm of matter in Gnosticism; there are only erroneous worldviews that regard the world of matter as a realm independent of the mind of God. In Gnosticism, when God regards the world as material, as created and not-God, then the Godhead ceases to know itself. In the final analysis, there is nothing for a Gnostic but God. Sophia, God's wisdom, is not a person distinct from God; Sophia is a form of God's own consciousness. When the Godhead ceases to know itself, God seems to be human and falls into the multiple personalities we know as human beings. Humankind is fallen God. The goal of Gnostic salvation, then, is to bring self-awareness back to God, which means that divine self-knowledge is the religious goal of human life.

Gnostic writers were haunted by the question, "How did the Godhead cease to know itself and begin to believe that God is human?" Gnostics believed that recollection of the origin of the difficulty in which God came to be would enable God (us) to return to correct self-apprehension. This is similar to the theory underlying psychoanalysis: that recollection or reexperience of an original trauma will dissolve that trauma. Salvation is the inversion of the myth of origin, a retracing upwards of the descent of God into the imprisoning world.

The Key to the Gnostic Religious Quest

In Gnosticism, the quest for individual self-knowledge by an aspect of God's mind is often termed the "fall of Wisdom" or the "fall of Sophia." This event is the key point in the Gnostic myth and in the Secret Book of John, for it is here that God began to disintegrate. Self-knowledge by an aspect of the mind cannot reveal the whole mind; one single aspect has no independent self to be known. God's wisdom imagined an objectively knowable self. God as an object of knowledge appeared, an objective demiurgic god ruling a new objective reality: a world apart from the mind of God. An aspect of God's mind, imagining objectivity, found knowledge of an imagined reality.

True introspection on the part of humans is a quest for self-understanding on the part of God, reversing the fall of God's wisdom into our human mode of consciousness. Enlightened human consciousness is Wisdom in the pleroma; normal human consciousness is Wisdom fallen and living in an illusory material world. Thus, there is no difference between psychotherapy for God and salvation for humans. Human beings are the state the Godhead finds itself in when God forgets who God is.

Self-knowledge is the key to the Gnostic religious quest, but not self-knowledge as an egocentric, personal, or individual matter. Rather, self-knowledge as the realization of our origin in God and our destiny to return there again. Egocentricity is a result of the arrogant attempt to know God as an object. Ego is a name for the continuing error that presents to the mind an external world. Projected outward, ego is demiurge, a false divine self, a false god. Insofar as there is an external world, there is an external god, indeed a vast series of gods, angels, demons, and archons. The panorama of unpleasant deity-demons found in Gnosticism is not reflective of their own doctrine, rather, it is the observation and analysis by the Gnostics of the religion of the Jews, Christians, and Pagans with whom they lived. Gnostics decided the god of the Hebrew Bible was no God at all but merely the incompetent creator of a world that never should have been created. Gnostics believed that ignorant people worshiped the ignorant being who commanded Adam never to eat from the tree of knowledge, the jealous god who falsely brags that he alone is God and there is no other God besides him. With spiritual insight, this God and the external world he is supposed to have created vanish.

Irenaeus tells us that Gnostics "confess that the Father of All contains all things, and that there is nothing whatsoever outside the pleroma."[1] This statement should be taken quite literally. The pleroma is the place of God's *sophia* (wisdom), *nous* (mind), *ennoia* (insight), *pronoia* (forethought), *logos* (reason), and so forth. In other words, the pleroma is the mind of God. Outside this there is nothing. What point is there in speaking of inside the pleroma at all then? Irenaeus writes that Gnostics "speak of what is outside and inside in reference to knowledge and ignorance, and not with respect to local distance; but that, in the pleroma or in those things which are contained by the Father, the whole creation which we know to have been formed ... is contained by the unspeakable greatness, as the center is in a circle."[2] Where then is the realm of matter, of ignorance, of alienation? Spatially, it is nowhere. Spatial terminology is ultimately inapplicable; Gnostics really speak only in terms of knowledge and ignorance.

The greatest Gnostic genius known to us, Valentinus, wrote in the Gospel of Truth about how it is that this external material world, constructed from oblivion, ignorance, and deficiency, has only false existence that vanishes instantly with knowledge:

> Since oblivion came into existence because the Father was not known, then if the Father comes to be known, oblivion will not exist from that moment on. This is the gospel of the one who is searched for, which was revealed to those who are perfect through the mercies of the Father—the hidden mystery, Jesus, the Christ. Through it he enlightened those in darkness…. Since the deficiency came into being because the Father was not known, therefore when the Father is known, from that moment on the deficiency will no longer exist. As with the ignorance of a person, when he comes to have knowledge his ignorance vanishes of itself as the darkness vanishes when light appears, so also the deficiency vanishes in the perfection. So from that moment on the form is not apparent, but it will vanish in the fusion of Unity, for now their works lie scattered. In time Unity will perfect the spaces. It is within Unity that each one will attain himself; within knowledge he will purify himself from multiplicity into Unity, consuming matter within himself like fire, and darkness by light, death by life.[3]

Here we have a beautiful statement of the final goal of the Gnostic religion, the resolution of multiplicity, matter, and darkness back into the One through the attainment of self-knowledge and self-realization by each human being.

The Metaphor of Mind

There appear to be two fundamental metaphors in religion, two basic ways that the divine reality can be modeled after human reality. The first is social-model religion; it is the model or set of metaphors with which we are most familiar. It underlies almost all nontheological and much theological discourse in Judaism, Islam, and Christianity and is at the heart of Western religion. God is said to be Father, King, or Judge. God sends messengers, passes judgment, rewards, and punishes. God loves and hates, is the inspiration for books, and for Christians can be depicted as a human being. All such ideas and metaphors are drawn from human social interaction. What is going on in the divine realm is said to be similar to what is going on in human society. God is the Lord and wants what a Lord would want by way of praise and adulation. What counts most is correct interpersonal behavior between God and humanity and between people in human society. There is nothing unusual about this model; it is the basis of virtually all of Western religion—Christian, Jewish, or Islamic.

The second metaphorical scheme is mind-model religion. The universe, the whole of reality, and especially the Divine are thought to be like a mind. Mental terms become the dominant form of metaphor. Key terms are *mind, word, wisdom, thought, reason,* and so forth. In this model, the nature of reality can best be known, indeed it can only be known, through introspection. Salvation comes through knowledge, insight, and meditation rather than through proper behavior, obedience, and agreement with established dogma.

Gnosticism is, essentially, a mind-model religion like Buddhism, Advaita Vedanta Hinduism, kabbalistic Judaism, and Sufism. The Gnostic ideas of cosmology as psychological evolution are similar to those of certain Eastern religions. The Samkhya philosophy as interpreted by Patanjali, author of the Yoga Sutras, claims that ignorance brings about the creation of what seems to be a world. Idealistic schools of Buddhism such as Zen and Tibetan Vajrayana teach that the world is brought into being as external materiality by the ignorance of persons who so perceive it. They claim that the Buddha-mind is all and everywhere and coextensive with the human mind. Kashmir Shaivism is very much like Gnosticism but with one crucial difference. It maintains that the Godhead (Shiva) deliberately forgot itself and became us in order to enjoy the splendor of discovering God again; Gnosticism regards that process as a tragedy growing out of a mistake.

Mythology is narrative, and narrative demands plot, places, and persons. Gnosticism's use of myth to communicate its main ideas led it into difficulty because there is a fundamental incompatibility between mind-model religion and social-model religion. The mind is not at all like a society and not at all like persons, social roles, or a series of spheres and chambers. The physics of mind is not the same as the physics of society. To use myth to communicate mind-model religion cannot help but cause confusion.

If we take the metaphor of mind seriously, we can see that Gnostics took upon themselves the incredible task of psychoanalyzing God. They did this work through introspection, presuming that since each awakened human is an aspect of God, undeluded self-knowledge is equivalent to knowledge of God. The career of the divine mind, its fall into illusion and self-forgetfulness, was not something independent of human existence but quite the contrary: because each individual is or has been the Godhead failing to know itself, each individual has as a personal history the fall of God.

The history of the cosmos is the history of God's mind, and this is the history of every individual. To break the "fall" and return to divine self-knowledge, Gnostics had to comprehend the process of their own fall into objectivity and alienation. It would be incumbent upon and therapeutic for Gnostics to rewrite the autobiography of God in their own language and to trace their own fall and return because Gnostic mythology is autobiography. It is the story of where we originated, how we came into this world, what our condition is now, and how we can escape. The savior is not a celestial being brought to earth; the savior is a capacity of mind, and the savior's journey from above is actually one's own insight journeying from within. Gnostic mythology derives from magical self-identification both with cosmic evolution and with the cosmic savior.

The Gospel of Philip claims:

> It is not possible for anyone to see anything of the things that actually exist unless he becomes like them. This is not the way with man in the world: he sees the sun without being a sun; and he sees the heaven and the earth and all other things, but he is not these things. This is quite in keeping with the truth. But you saw something of that place and you became those things. You saw the Spirit; you became Spirit.

> You saw Christ; you became Christ. You saw the Father; you shall become the Father. In this place you see everything and do not see yourself, but in that place you do see yourself—and what you see you shall become.[4]

Such passages show that in Gnosticism, the distinction between savior and saved ceases to exist. In Gnosticism, you must save yourself and in so doing save God.

The Secret Book of John

Gnostic ideas are expressed in mythology and psychology simultaneously. This results in substantial confusion because components of mind certainly don't act like individual beings in a social system, even though the mythological form of expression requires this. Confusion is compounded by the imaginative creativity of Gnostic authors who felt free to rewrite myth to include their own unique insights. And yet we need not despair. The overall story and theory of the Secret Book of John are reasonably comprehensible. Even if the details, names, and categories that arise in the work don't all fit neatly together, that is usual for mythologies. In the case of the Secret Book of John, the variations that make the book difficult to follow are a testimony to its great influence. Each of the texts of the Secret Book of John that we now have incorporates bits from different versions of the book, as centuries of work by scribes and translators introduced comments, variants, explanatory summaries, and Christian dialogues into a book that originally lacked them. The present book will help you to follow the story of God as the Secret Book of John presents it. As long as you are willing to let the text go off on its various tangents and deviate from the main story without demanding a consistent and clear narrative, you will be able to understand the book and its main messages.

There have been several translations of the Secret Book of John into English and this version is indebted to all of them. It is fundamentally based on the excellent interlinear translation of Michael Grondin. It has been influenced by and has benefited from the following translations:

Soren Giversen's in his book, *Apocryphon Johannis* (Copenhagen: Prostant Apud Munksgaard, 1963); Frederik Wisse's in *The Nag Hammadi Library in English* (San Francisco: HarperSanFrancisco, 1978); Bentley Layton's in his book, *The Gnostic Scriptures* (New York: Doubleday, 1987); Howard N. Bream's in his book, *The Apocryphon of John and Other Coptic Translations* (Baltimore: Halgo, 1987); and Marvin Meyer's in his book, *The Gnostic Bible* (Boston: Shambhala, 2003).

Ancient books were written without separations between words; the letters just march on and on across each written page. Ancient scribes had nothing comparable to our system of punctuation marks, paragraphs, and so forth. In converting the Secret Book of John into English, I have rendered the text with English punctuation and divided it into many separate sections using a broken-line poetic style. I have sometimes distinguished what appear to be scribal comments added to the text by putting them in square brackets. My own clarifications about the translation have been inserted in curved parentheses and in a different font throughout. The Secret Book of John was compiled from at least five different types of material: a Christian introduction, conclusion, and dialogue about the fate of the soul; a Middle-Platonic discourse on the One; a long and complex Jewish-Gnostic myth; a section of a magical book attributed to Zoroaster; and a hymn about the descent of Providence into this world. If you expect the text to be a seamless whole that reads nicely from beginning to end, you will have a difficult time with it. Understanding it to be a woven tapestry of diverse parts that sometimes cohere well, and at other times are discordant, will make it easier to comprehend.

Gnosticism Today

In this "New Age" and new millennium, the ancient religion of the Gnostics is returning to life. Scholarship on Gnosticism by prominent academics such as Elaine Pagels appears on best-seller lists. During Christian holidays, television programs often discuss the ancient Gnostic texts and claim to reveal their mysteries and secrets. Popular novels such as

The Da Vinci Code are based, in part, on the discovery of the Nag Hammadi Gnostic Gospels. As time goes on, more and more people find pleasure in the strange and novel ideas of the Gnostic thinkers who lived two millennia ago.

Gnosticism attracts so much present-day interest because, in a strange way, it is a quite modern form of religion. Gnosticism insists that we should seek divinity within ourselves and assures us that we are ultimately divine. Gnostic texts take a firmly positive view of human beings, looking at the "fall into sin" as the failure to realize our divinity rather than as a descent into moral incompetence. Although assuming the need for a basically moral life, Gnosticism is not a moralistic religion and has no place for a god of judgment, sentencing people to an eternity of bliss or torment. Gnosticism is individualistic; we all need to discover our own divine self-awareness and not rely on church or priests for our spiritual growth. The experiences of self-discovery and spiritual ascent are crucial to Gnosticism. This self-affirming, individualistic religion fits well with the values of modern secular culture.

Gnosticism was never very good at being an "organized" religion, which is one reason why Christian orthodoxy was able to use police power to destroy it. Instead of insisting upon a mandated list of approved scriptures, Gnosticism encouraged creativity, imagination, invention, and novelty. Irenaeus reported that, "every one of them generates something new, day by day, according to his ability. No one of them is deemed perfect who does not develop among them some mighty fictions."[5] Today, in many circles, such imaginative inventiveness is admired rather than held in contempt. Gnostic creativity did not, however, just come up with utterly new systems of comprehending the world; it tended to work within a fundamental mythological structure. While individual authors changed details, names, divine personages, and mythic events quite liberally, they did so in accordance with that set of ideas. The fundamental structure of the Gnostic myth is found in its basic form in the Secret Book of John, the most important and valued book that the Gnostic religion ever produced.

Timeline

(all dates approximate CE)

33 ——————— Jesus of Nazareth crucified

49 ——————— Paul's first letter to the Thessalonians

60 ——————— Paul's letter to the Romans
65 ——————— Q Gospel (the source of sayings used by Matthew and Luke)
70 ——————— Gospel of Thomas
             Gospel of Mark
80 ——————— Gospel of Matthew
85 ——————— *First edition of the Secret Book of John*
90 ——————— Gospel of Luke—Acts of the Apostles
95 ——————— Gospel of John
             Revelation to John

110 —————— Pastoral Epistles

120 —————— *Second (Christianized) edition of the Secret Book of John*

180 —————— Irenaeus writes *Against Heresies*

The Secret
Book of John
The Gnostic Gospel

❖ The Secret Book of John, like most of the texts found at Nag Hammadi, concludes with a title: "The Apocryphon of John." An apocryphon is a secret or hidden book. This title might remind you of Paul's statement in First Corinthians 2:7: "We speak God's wisdom, mysterious, hidden, which God predetermined before time for our glory."

1 Since the book's present title, "The Secret Book of John," presupposes a Christian orientation (as being related to Jesus's disciple John), but the book initially was not Christian, it certainly had some other title when it first circulated. The original title may have been "The Revelation of the Mysteries Hidden in Silence." Then, when a Christian redesigned the book to be a revelation by Jesus, its title was framed by the phrases, "The Teaching of the Savior ... Those Things That He Taught to John, His Disciple."

The Teaching of the Savior
The Revelation of the Mysteries
Hidden in Silence[1]
Those Things That He Taught to John, His Disciple.

❖ This dialogue between Jesus and John seems to have been added on to an older, non-Christian Jewish-Gnostic text in order to turn the Secret Book of John into a Christian revelation.

1 The present scene takes place in the vicinity of the Jerusalem Temple after Jesus's crucifixion and ascension. James and John, the sons of Zebedee, are mentioned in the New Testament gospels. They are two of Jesus's twelve disciples; Jesus nicknames them "Boanerges" meaning "Sons of Thunder" (Mark 3:17; Matthew 10:2).

2 The Pharisee called Arimanios has a name that is unknown in the Bible or any other early Jewish source. It probably comes from the Zoroastrian tradition, a Persian religion that featured a vision of conflict between a God of Good (Ahura Mazda) and a force for evil named Ahriman. Accordingly, the name Arimanios signifies the Pharisee's wicked nature.

3 The whole Gospel of John is summarized at 16:28 where Jesus says, "I came from the Father into the world, now I am leaving the world and returning to the Father," an idea that is reflected here in John's reply.

4 John's retreat to a deserted mountainous place to sort out his feelings is similar to Jesus's venture into the desert immediately after the Spirit came to him at his baptism.

5 These questions reflect principal themes of the Secret Book of John, which begins by teaching about the nature of the Father, then describes the nature and origin of the realm to which saved people will go, and finally narrates the cosmic crisis that made the journey of the Savior into the world necessary.

☐ Prologue

One day John, the brother of James (these are the sons of Zebedee), was going up to the Temple.[1] A Pharisee by the name of Arimanios came up to him and challenged him, asking: "Where is the teacher you used to follow?"[2]

John replied, "He has gone back to the place from which he came."[3]

The Pharisee said, "That Nazarene misled you (plural), told you lies, closed your hearts and turned you away from your ancestral traditions."

When I heard these things, I, John, turned away from the temple and went off to a deserted mountainous place.[4] I was very unhappy, saying to myself:

"How was the Savior designated?

Why did his Father send him into the world?

Who is his Father?

What kind of realm will we go to?[5]

For, although he told us 'This realm is modeled on the imperishable realm,'

He didn't teach us about the latter."

(continued on page 7)

6   Now John apprehends the Savior in his transcendent forms. As in the account of Jesus's baptism, here too the heavens open. The shaking of the world indicates that the created lower order of things—this world—is impermanent, threatened by revelation, and ultimately doomed to be destroyed by reabsorption into the higher realms. When divine Providence appears as revealer in the Secret Book of John's concluding poem, creation shakes.

7   The idea that the Lord appears in a variety of forms and guises in his self-revelation was not uncommon in the second century CE. In the Acts of Peter, from the later second century CE, Peter says that he "with the sons of Zebedee" saw such brightness as made them fall as if dead and that they heard an indescribable voice and thought themselves blinded by the brightness. A little later, Peter tells the story of old, blind Christian widows who were given sight by such brightness: "They said: 'We saw an old man of such comeliness as we are not able to declare to you; but others said: We saw a young man; and others: We saw a boy touching our eyes delicately, and so were our eyes opened.'"

8   Jesus's question may refer to Matthew 28:17, where some of his disciples doubt the risen Christ.

All of a sudden, while I was contemplating these
   things,
      Behold!
The heavens opened and the whole of creation shone
   with a light from above,
      And the world quaked![6]
I was afraid, yet
      Behold!
A little child appeared before me in the light.
   I continued looking at him, as he became an old
      man
         And then he changed again, becoming like a
            young man.
   I didn't understand what I was seeing,
         But the one likeness had several forms in the
            light,
         And those likenesses appeared each through the
            other
         And the vision had three forms.[7]

He said to me,
   "John, why doubt?[8]
   Why be afraid?
   Don't you know this image?

(continued on page 9)

9 The phrase "I am with you always" is the last sentence of Matthew's Gospel (28:20), spoken by the risen Christ to his disciples.

10 In Greek, the word for "spirit," *pneuma,* is neuter in grammatical gender while the Latin *spiritus* is masculine. Therefore, in Western theology, while Father and Son are masculine, the gender of the Holy Spirit is unclear, although regularly referred to with the masculine pronoun *he.* However, in Aramaic, Hebrew, and Syriac, the word for "spirit" is feminine in grammatical gender. Accordingly, in early Syriac Christianity (and probably also in the Aramaic Christianity of Jesus) the Holy Spirit was conceived to be a feminine being, the Mother. In those Eastern Christian churches the trinity could have been "Father, Mother, and Son."

11 The Secret Book of John claims to reveal Jesus's teachings about what is, was, and will be, and so give a record of mythological time, the nature of the present world, and the path to salvation that should be followed in the future. The intended audience of the whole revelation is "the immovable race of the perfect humanity" whom we might call "the saved," or in the present context, "true Christians." Their being "immovable" contrasts them with the changeable present world. Their true home is in the world beyond this world.

❖ Here the added Christian dialogue section ends. The older section of the Secret Book of John will begin with a Middle-Platonic discussion of the Incomprehensible One.

Be not afraid.
　　I am with you (plural) always.[9]
　　I am the Father
　　　　The Mother
　　　　　　The Son[10]
　　I am the incorruptible
　　　　Purity.

I have come to teach you
　　About what is
　　And what was
　　And what will be
　　In order for you to understand
　　　　The invisible world
　　　　And the world that is visible
　　　　And the immovable race of perfect humanity.[11]

Raise your head;
Understand my lessons;
Share them with any others who have received the
　　Spirit,
　　　　Who are from the immovable race of perfect
　　　　　　humanity."

❖ The introduction is over. Here the revelation begins with the ultimate reality: the Platonic One. It would not be wrong to think here of the Brahman of Hindu philosophy: that from which all reality flows and which is, in the final analysis, the only reality there is. Note that this is philosophical monism; that is, that there is, in ultimate reality, only one being. As the text goes on, it will advocate the position of philosophical idealism, postulating that divine mental reality is all the reality there is and that the external material world is a mistaken notion. Ironically, many people, even scholars who should know better, declare that Gnosticism is a dualism based on two fundamental and opposed principles. Here we have the primary Gnostic text spelling out an anti-dualistic perspective as strongly as it can. The world does apparently become dualistic later on, but only by mistake; the ultimate fate of the world is to be monistic as it was in the beginning.

1 The main metaphorical descriptor for the One is "light," which connects back to the first instant of revelation to John when he is blinded by light.

2 The Secret Book of John takes pains to insist that the One is beyond description, literally inconceivable. No words are adequate to describe it. To say, for example, that the One is properly described with the word *God* is wrong. No words are adequate. It is more than anything you can think or say.

❖ The One is completely independent. It is the ultimate starting point, a pure point without dimension. It is what there was a microsecond before the big bang thirteen and a half billion years ago, with everything existing in it but it existing in nothing because nothing is all that has come into being so far.

☐ The Inexpressible One

The One rules all. Nothing has authority over it.
   It is the God.
   It is Father of everything,
         Holy One
         The invisible one over everything.
   It is uncontaminated
         Pure light no eye can bear to look within.[1]
The One is the Invisible Spirit.
   It is not right to think of it as a God or as like God.
   It is more than just God.[2]

Nothing is above it.
Nothing rules it.
   Since everything exists within it
         It does not exist within anything.

(continued on page 13)

11

3 │ Although the Secret Book of John is sometimes mythological (speaking of concepts as individuals), and sometimes ontological (concerned with the being of things), it is consistently psychological, concerned with the unfolding of the mind of God. Here God exists in a state prior to self-consciousness. It is, as Brahman is in the Upanishads, pure *sat* (being), *chit* (consciousness), *ananda* (bliss), and nothing else. Not only do humans have no capacity to know it, it does not yet know itself.

❖ │ Theologians have long observed that if God is beyond all human language, then God cannot be described or discussed. But if God cannot be described or discussed, how can human beings proceed to know God? All knowledge must ultimately be inadequate. In these verses the Secret Book of John acknowledges the futility of human language and conceptualization to encompass the One for whom even the term *God* is insufficient.

4 │ Platonic philosophy was widespread and very influential in the ancient world. The use of *the One* as terminology for the highest divine principle arises from Platonism and was often used by Neoplatonic philosophers such as Plotinus, who lived perhaps a century after the Secret Book of John was written.

5 │ The argument here is that the One in its perfect state is logically beyond all knowledge, comprehension, and understanding. Such words imply a second being to have the knowledge, do the comprehending, and achieve the understanding, but there is no second being if the One is all.

Since it is not dependent on anything
    It is eternal.[3]
It is absolutely complete and so needs nothing.
It is utterly perfect
Light.

The One is without boundaries[4]
    Nothing exists outside of it to border it
The One cannot be investigated
    Nothing exists apart from it to investigate it
The One cannot be measured
    Nothing exists external to it to measure it

The One cannot be seen
    For no one can envision it
The One is eternal
    For it exists forever
The One is inconceivable
    For no one can comprehend it
The One is indescribable
    For no one can put any words to it.[5]

The One is infinite light
    Purity
    Holiness
        Stainless,
The One is incomprehensible
    Perfectly free from corruption.

(continued on page 15)

6   This line of thought is what is called negative theology and can be traced back at least to Plato's Parminides (380 BCE). To say that God is "not perfect" is not to claim that God is imperfect but rather to deny that whatever concept you have in your mind regarding the meaning of *perfect* is adequate. Similarly, whatever you think of when you think *divine* is less than what God truly is and, accordingly, God is not "divine." This is a discussion of the adequacy of language, not of God, per se. God cannot be discussed. Buddhist texts often take this same approach in regard to nirvana, declaring its inexpressible, inconceivable nature and the inadequacy of language to discuss it.

7   Just as you cannot say God is "divine," you cannot say God is "physical." Having suggested that the One is not whatever a human word would have it be, the text goes on to offer another linguistic ploy. God both is (in some ways) and is not (in some ways) what human words would declare. In some ways God is physical, in some ways not, or, to use double negatives, God is neither physical nor unphysical. Again, the discussion here is not about the nature of God, but about the nature of human language and its inadequacy in describing and discussing God. "Not this, not that," the Upanishads say about Brahman: *neti, neti*.

8   The philosopher Ludwig Wittgenstein famously said: "Wovon man nicht sprechen kann, daruber muss man schweigen," which means, "That about which one cannot speak, about that one must be silent." But, of course, theologians and mystics in both Eastern and Western traditions have recognized for millennia both that their language is inadequate and that they must nevertheless speak. Perfect discussion of God takes place in silence and so the Secret Book of John begins by describing its contents as "The Revelation of the Mysteries Hidden in Silence."

Not "perfect"
Not "blessed"
Not "divine"
But superior to such concepts.[6]
    Neither physical nor unphysical
    Neither immense nor infinitesimal[7]
    It is impossible to specify in quantity or quality
        For it is beyond knowledge.[8]

(continued on page 17)

9 │ The German philosopher Martin Heidegger wrote that "das Sein des Seienden 'ist' nicht selbst ein Seiendes," meaning that "the Being of beings is not itself a being." That is one of the ideas the Secret Book of John is trying to communicate; the One is not a kind of being, but the underlying reality that sustains all being.

10 │ The One is superior to all, although one must remember that the human word *superior* is inadequate. The One transcends all conceptual categories, all categories of being and of time. There is as yet no being or time or space, for there is nowhere and no time outside of the One. There is no outside or inside of the One.

11 │ At this point in the text, we are still reading about the state of affairs before the big bang, when any notion of time is meaningless. But the next stage in the development of reality is about to take place. There is a hint of events to come in the notion of the One apprehending itself in its own light. Is the One that apprehends the same as the One who is apprehended?

12 │ We hear now of the realm of the One and of the realms within that realm. Some sort of structure is hinted at. The One is taking on form, however silent and incomprehensible it may be. The word *realm* is the translation of the Greek *aeon* that is often retained in the Coptic version of the Secret Book of John. The word *aeon* implies eternal time. It can mean a power existing from eternity: an emanation of God and, therefore, a functional component of God. As such, it is a psychic space within the mind of God. Though the word *realm* is used here, there is really no single word that captures the full meaning of the text. You simply have to develop a sophisticated notion of what a "realm" functioning within the mind of God might be.

The One is not a being among other beings[9]
   It is vastly superior
      But it is not "superior."
It is outside of realms of being and time
   For whatever is within realms of being was created
   And whatever is within time had time allotted to it[10]
The One receives nothing from anything.
   It simply apprehends itself in its own perfect light.[11]

The One is majestic.
   The One is measureless majesty,
Chief of all Realms
     Producing all realms[12]
Light
   Producing light
Life
   Producing life
Blessedness
   Producing blessedness
Knowledge
   Producing knowledge
Good
   Producing goodness
Mercy
   Producing mercy

(continued on page 19)

13 We are back now to language, to words being used in reference to the One. But it is not appropriate to apply such words as *life, blessedness,* and *knowledge* to the One as if they were adequate categorizations. Rather, it is better to think of such things as proceeding from the One but not constituting aspects of the One itself, implying that there is a possibility of existence beyond the Incomprehensible One. Into that possibility, later into all reality, the One sends forth generosity, mercy, goodness, and so forth. This is in accordance with Middle-Platonic philosophy.

14 The principle production of the One is "light," to be thought of as a metaphor for whatever exists beyond the central dimensionless space of the One itself. That light is beyond comprehension. This is supernal light, the light that Genesis speaks of prior to the creation of the sun and moon and stars.

Generosity
    Producing generosity[13]
        [It does not "possess" these things.]

It gives forth light beyond measure, beyond
    comprehension.[14]
        [What can I say?]
His realm is eternal, peaceful, silent, resting, before
    everything.
He is the head of every realm sustaining each of them
    through goodness.

1 The comment in brackets appears to have been added to an earlier version of the Secret Book of John. This happens often in the document because it went through many hands and revisions in its history. It is not always possible to separate out comments added by scribes and editors from the original text itself. This particular passage refers back to the opening stanzas where the Savior provides a "revelation of the mysteries" to John. Logically, if the One is beyond comprehension, only if it reveals itself can anything of it be known.

2 Now the Secret Book of John changes from a Platonic discussion of the nature of the One and the inadequacies of human language to a discussion of creation. How is it possible that from the One this complex material world emerges? The beginning of differentiation between the One and anything else—the instant of the big bang in this Gnostic cosmology—takes place when the One achieves self-reflective self-consciousness. Prior to this, the One was just consciousness, period. Now it perceives itself. It takes on more of a mythological character as an actor in the play of developing reality; it is the Father. He apprehends himself in his light but what he apprehends and he himself are not strictly identical. The knower is not identical with the known. His consciousness of himself as image gives rise to an emotional reaction, for he is "enamored of the image he sees," similar to the way Narcissus fell in love with his own image reflected in the water. The image of the One will become the heavenly world; the image of the heavenly world will become the world below.

3 We have a conflux of two metaphors here: the Father surrounded by light and the Father surrounded by water. These are probably two different poetic traditions of mythological description that the Secret Book of John is affirming simultaneously.

☐ The Origin of Reality

[We would know nothing of the ineffable
And nothing of the immeasurable
Without the help of the one who comes forth
    from the One who is the Father.
He alone has informed us.][1]

The Father is surrounded by light.
    He apprehends himself in that light,
    [Which is the pure spring of the water of life that
      sustains all realms].
He is conscious of his image everywhere around him,
    Perceiving his image in this spring of Spirit
        Pouring forth from himself.
He is enamored of the image he sees in the light-
  water,[2]
    The spring of pure light-water enveloping him.[3]

(continued on page 23)

4 The One has become Two. This is a psychological process, not a process of material creation. The Father has perceived his own image within his own light and that act of perception—that awareness of himself—has come into being as a provisionally separate entity. The text is undecided whether to call the self-conscious awareness of the One its *ennoia* ("thought" or insight") or its *pronoia* ("providence"). While we might wish that there would be clear distinctions in the text's use of psychological terminology, the text seems happy to regard such terms as synonyms. Now the self-awareness of the Father presents itself and assumes a mythological role. She (ennoia/pronoia) is like the Father, but a reflection of him rather than the perfect original. Inherent in this reflected image is the entirety of God; it is God's self-consciousness. In the words of the New Testament's letter to the Colossians: "the image of the invisible God, the firstborn of all creation. In him were created all things in heaven and earth ..." (1:15–19). You should try to bear in mind throughout the Secret Book of John that all of the various beings that come forth are ultimately aspects of one mind. Just as your own psychological functions of thought and memory and perception aren't separate beings but are part of you, so forms of the Father's awareness remain part of the Father.

5 The Greek word *pronoia,* meaning "forethought," is used here for the mythological character of God's self-awareness. *Pronoia* was a common word in philosophical and psychological speculations of the time. An equivalent translation with a Latin origin is "providence" or "foresight." *Forethought* is a word that has no particular resonance in English, so I use the word *providence* for *pronoia*. There is a Christian theological tradition behind the idea of God's Providence; it means God's plan for salvation. It means that here too.

His self-aware thought (Ennoia) came into being,
   Appearing to him in the effulgence of his light.
She stood before him.[4]
This, then, is the first of the powers, prior to
   everything,
Arising out of the mind of the Father
   The Providence (Pronoia) of everything.[5]
   Her light reflects his light.

(continued on page 25)

6 The One is becoming more of a mythological character in this passage, too. He is Father and he is the Invisible Spirit. Providence is the "image of the invisible" and is one notch lower in the sequence of divine realms. The "Virgin Spirit" and the "Invisible Spirit" are synonyms for "the Father." Because the Secret Book of John emerges from a long tradition of texts and speculations, many of which have influenced its language, we often find multiple and sometimes inconsistent terms used to refer to the same beings. The word *Virgin* shows that the Father requires no consort or partner for his creative emanations; all other factors must work through a partner or their emanation will be chaotic.

7 Providence is Barbelo. Many scholars have suggested origins for the word *Barbelo,* deriving it variously from the Hebrew, the Coptic, and the Greek, but no suggestion has won general approval. It is a proper name, not a psychological or philosophical term. As the Secret Book of John moves along, it becomes increasingly mythological, turning from conceiving the universe as the structure of the mind of the One toward describing the universe as a cosmic drama wherein supernatural actors play humanlike roles. The introduction of the name Barbelo stands at the beginning of that process.

8 Barbelo standing before the Virgin Spirit, glorifying him and praising him is an image that stems from the idea of a heavenly court. It is not a specifically Jewish idea, but the Hebrew Bible certainly depicts Yahweh enthroned among the angels, the seraphim and cherubim, receiving their glorification and praise. Here the Father's celestial court is beginning to take shape in the Secret Book of John, an example of how the social model of religion is used to describe a mental model of divine reality.

9 Notice the redundancy of this sentence. It is a comment on the text that has been included in the text, probably by a copyist scribe. Such comments are quite common and often, as here, serve to remind readers of what they would already know if they had been paying any attention at all.

She is from his image in his light
  Perfect in power
  Image of the invisible perfect Virgin Spirit.[6]
She is the initial power
  glory of Barbelo[7]
  glorious among the realms
  glory of revelation.
She gave glory to the Virgin Spirit
She praised him
  For she arose from him.[8]
[This, the first Thought, is the Spirit's image.][9]

(continued on page 27)

10 Barbelo is given a whole host of names. The popularity and influence of the Secret Book of John within Gnostic circles was so great that many versions and variations came into being, some of which have been preserved. These variations often use different names for the same mythological beings and here a series of variant names are given for the same mythic person.

11 In the language of the Secret Book of John, the word *thrice* forms superlatives. So rather than saying Barbelo is "most male" as we would in English, "thrice male" is used. In the Hermetic Egyptian tradition, Hermes was called thrice great Hermes or Hermes Trismegistos.

12 The gender of words here and elsewhere in the Secret Book of John must not be taken seriously. Barbelo is Mother, First Man, Thrice Male, and so forth. But "her" sex is just a mythological convenience; "she" is the productive interface between the One and "his" court of mental powers and, as such, she is "the universal womb" and so, called female. But within the more important psychological set of mythic events, "she" is the self-awareness of the One come into semi-independent being. To attribute a particular sex to self-awareness and take it literally would be foolish; the text's inconsistency in these matters is a sign that the author is not taking such sexual designations seriously at all. Calling her androgynous is a good indication that no literal sexuality is intended.

She is the universal womb
    She is before everything
She is:
    Mother-Father
    First Man
    Holy Spirit[10]

    Thrice Male
    Thrice Powerful
    Thrice Named[11]

Androgynous eternal realm
First to arise among the invisible realms.[12]

❖ The pleroma (or fullness) begins to come into being in this sequence. The pleroma is the aeon, or realm, of Barbelo. It is, however, not a particular place or court of celestial beings, even though it is described that way. It is the mind of God expanding from its initial self-knowledge. The first movement is self-reflective, self-conscious thought (signified as the Mother or Barbelo). The second movement, taking place here, is the differentiation of self-consciousness into forms and types of consciousness, into various mental powers. The process by which each comes into being is similar:

1. Self-awareness asks consciousness (Barbelo asks the Virgin Spirit / Invisible Spirit)

2. Consciousness agrees

3. The power comes forth

4. The power stands

5. The power gives glory to consciousness and self-awareness (Barbelo and the Virgin Spirit / Invisible Spirit)

As the mythological tale unfolds we are evidently to imagine a celestial court made up of superior and subordinate beings standing and glorifying a central being.

❖ The arrangement of these beings reminds one of the form of the mandala used to symbolize the unity of mental forces in the Tibetan Buddhist tradition.

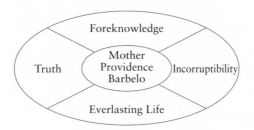

☐ Primary Structures of the Divine Mind

She, Barbelo, asked the Virgin Spirit for Foreknowledge
(prognosis).
   The Spirit agreed.
   Foreknowledge came forth and stood by Providence
   [This one came through the Invisible Virgin Spirit's
      Thought.]
   Foreknowledge gave glory to the Spirit
      And to Barbelo, the Spirit's perfect power,
      For she was the reason that it had come into
         being.

She, Barbelo, asked the Virgin Spirit for Incorruptibility.
   The Spirit agreed.
   Incorruptibility came forth and stood by Thought
      and Foreknowledge.
   Incorruptibility gave glory to the Invisible Virgin
      Spirit
      And to Barbelo,
      For she was the reason that it had come into
         being.

(continued on page 31)

1 We have come to a significant development. The whole of the realm of Providence, which is the pleroma, is defined as the First Man, a fact that later takes on tremendous significance. The whole pleroma will be displayed later in the Secret Book of John to lower powers who will model the first human being, Adam, upon it. So this is the prototypical human, the First Man, the primordial perfection of which humanity is a reflection.

2 This sequence of synonyms implies, reasonably enough, that the fivefold expansion of Providence into pleroma does not result in a host of different beings but rather a system of different potentialities within the one Thought. And what is that Thought, but the Father envisioning Himself.

She asked for Everlasting Life.
  The Spirit agreed.
  Everlasting Life came forth and they all stood
    together.
  They gave glory to the Invisible Spirit
      And to Barbelo,
      For she was the reason that it had come into
        being.

She asked for Truth.
  The Spirit agreed.
  Truth came forth and they all stood together.
  They gave glory to the Invisible Spirit
      And to Barbelo,
      For she was the reason that it had come into
        being.

This is the fivefold realm of the Father:
  The First Man[1]
      Who is the Image of the Invisible Spirit
      Who is Providence
      Who is Barbelo
      Who is Thought[2]

(continued on page 33)

3 The idea of the mandala of five within the pleroma really being ten—an androgynous realm—is similar to the Tibetan Buddhist idea that each mental power depicted within a mandala has both a wisdom and a compassion aspect. The former is feminine, the latter masculine, and the combination of both is essential for psychic development. Thus, many mandalas depict the psychic powers as buddhas, or bodhisattvahs, in *yab-yum* sexual union position, combining the masculine and feminine aspect. It is this sort of symbolism that the Secret Book of John presupposes at this point. All five of the revealed beings are feminine gender terms in the Greek language; therefore, to complete the androgynous realm, their five counterparts would have been labeled with masculine gender words, but those words are not revealed here.

And
Foreknowledge-Incorruptibility-Life Everlasting-
Truth.

[These are an androgynous fivefold realm—therefore it
is a realm of ten—of the Father.][3]

1 The Secret Book of John uses increasingly mythological language as it develops its vision of the origin of the world. Imagery of sexual intercourse begins here with the Father impregnating Barbelo with a glance. Barbelo gives birth to a spark of light, a reflection of her own nature as the light-image surrounding the Father.

2 This new third being is distinctly inferior to the Father and the Mother, with inferior blessedness. He is their only child, their only begotten Son, a phrase with which many Christians are very familiar thanks to its use in John 3:16 where "God so loved the world that He gave his only begotten Son." This child is the completion of the primordial trinity: Father, Mother, and Son. The only begotten Son is "light," an idea that brings to mind Jesus's saying number 77 in the Gospel of Thomas, "I am the light above everything," and in the Gospel of John 14:6, "I am the way, the truth, and the light."

3 A second set of structures is beginning to come into being: the first—Barbelo—was within Providence, the second now is within the Son. The whole passage echoes with a play on words. The word *anointing* is the foundation of the word *Christ,* or "the anointed one," which is *Christos* in Greek. The word for "goodness," retained here in the Greek, is *chrestotes;* to say that Christ is good would be to say that Christos is chrestos.

Secondary Structures of the Divine Mind

The Father looked into Barbelo
    [into the pure light surrounding the Invisible Spirit]
Barbelo conceived and bore a spark of light[1]
    Who had blessedness similar to, but not equal to,
      her blessedness,
    Who was the only child of that mother-father
        The only offspring,
        The only begotten child of the pure light, the
          Father.[2]

The Invisible Virgin Spirit celebrated the light that had
    been produced
    Coming forth from the first power who is
        The Providence
        Barbelo.

The Spirit anointed him with Goodness, making him
    perfect.
        [He lacked no goodness whatsoever,
        for he was anointed with the Invisible Spirit's
          Goodness][3]

(continued on page 37)

4　The Son's reception of something—presumably a spirit of goodness—that is "poured upon him" may bring to mind Jesus's receiving the Holy Spirit. Luke's Gospel speaks of Jesus being "anointed with the spirit" (4:18). It was surely inevitable that this "only begotten" Son, who is the anointed one receiving the Spirit, would have been identified in the early days of Christianity with Jesus Christ.

5　The emergence of Goodness and Mind begin the description of the internal structure of the Son who, we must bear in mind, is not an individual person but a component set of structures within the whole aeon, or realm, of God. And that, in turn, may be conceived of as the fullness, the pleroma, of the mind of God.

❖　Here the relatively clear structuring of the mythological creation of the mind of God becomes fuzzy. The point seems to be that after the emergence of Goodness and Mind there came Word and Will to form a fourfold structure akin to the fourfold structure within Barbelo. Mind and Will, from the structure of the Son, pair up with Everlasting Life and Foreknowledge from the structure of the Mother. This pairing allows for the construction of a reasonably comprehensive multilevel mandala depicting the whole of the heavenly realm.

He stood in the Spirit's presence and it was poured
  upon him.
Having received this anointing from the Spirit he
  immediately glorified him
    And he glorified the perfect Providence.
    Because of her he had come into being.[4]

He asked for Mind (nous) to be a companion to him.
    The Spirit consented.
        When the Invisible Spirit consented
    Mind came into being.
        It stood by the Anointed and glorified the Spirit
        and Barbelo.[5]

These beings came into existence through silence and
  thought.

He wished to act through the word of the Invisible
  Spirit.
    Whose will became an action and appeared with
      Mind
        Glorifying the Light.

And then Word followed Will into being.

(continued on page 39)

6 The application of the term *autogenes* to the Son is baffling. The word *autogenes* comes from *auto* which means "self-alone," and *genes,* which means "generated," "begotten," "created," or "born." It is quite clear that the Son comes into being through the interaction of Father and Mother (or the Invisible Spirit and Barbelo depending on your preferred vocabulary) and so the Son is *not* autogenes. The very notion of him as the "only begotten Son of the pure light, the Father" contradicts the idea that he is self begotten, and yet "autogenes" is a prominent description of him; no translation of it will be attempted here.

❖ The mandala presented in regard to the Son is as follows:

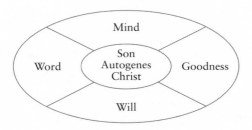

[The Christ, the Divine Autogenes, created
  everything through the Word.]6

Everlasting Life and Will,
Mind and Foreknowledge
  Stood together.
  They glorified the Invisible Spirit and Barbelo.
  Because of her they had come into being.

1 | According to orthodox Christianity, Jesus, God's son, has been given power and dominion over everything. In many churches today the Lord's Prayer concludes with the phrase (from Daniel 7:14) "for thine is the Kingdom and the Power and the Glory forever." Here the text of the Secret Book of John credits the divine Son and Christ with such authority, as does Matthew 28:18, where Jesus himself declares: "All power in heaven and earth has been given to me." It is possible, although far from certain, that the attribution of such overwhelming cosmic power to the man Jesus, whom Christians declared to be the Son of God, derives from an earlier Gnostic tradition of attributing such power to the cosmic figure of the only begotten Son, the Autogenes.

2 | The Secret Book of John is to be shared, we were told, only with those of "the immovable race." The highest name of all goes only to those "worthy to hear it," and it is not given in the manuscript. Presumably the highest name is associated with the Son, and not the Father, because we have been instructed in considerable detail that no nomenclature is possible for that infinitely Incomprehensible One.

☐ Tertiary Structures of the Divine Mind

The Holy Spirit
Brought his and Barbelo's divine autogenes Son to
  completion
    In order that he could stand before the great
      Invisible Virgin Spirit
        As the divine autogenes Christ
      And honor him with a mighty voice.

[The Son came through Providence.]

The Invisible Spirit
Placed the Divine Autogenes over everything.
  All authorities were subordinated to him;[1]
  The truth within him let him learn everything.

[He is called by the highest name of all.
That name will be told only to those who are
  worthy to hear it.][2]

(continued on page 43)

3 | Christ is a spark of infinite divine light. From that light emerge four lights bearing specific names: a set of beings who appear with surprising frequency in Gnostic accounts of the origin of the world. They seem to have the role of angels and to be individual beings rather than specific characteristics of the divine mind as the other revealed beings were.

4 | No one can be sure what the names of the four lights mean. It is most likely that all of them originated as Hebrew words having reference to illumination in connection with God, who is *El,* in Hebrew. But then what of the name Daveithai, which seems to originate from David? No one knows. Soren Giversen suggests the following in his book *Apocryphon Johannis:* Harmozel may mean "Standing Light"; Oriel surely means "God's Light"; Daveithai possibly means "of David"; and Eleleth may mean "Morning Star."

From the light, which is the Christ,
From the incorruptibility,
    Through a gift of the Spirit
The four lights arising from the Divine Autogenes
    stood before him.[3]

[The four fundamental powers are Understanding,
    Grace, Perception, and Consideration.]

Grace exists within the realm of the light called
    Harmozel, the first angel.[4]
    Along with Harmozel are
Grace
Truth
Form.

The second light is called Oriel and it stands over
    the second realm.
    With Oriel are
Conceptualization (Epinoia)
Perception
Memory.

(continued on page 45)

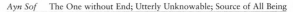

Ayn Sof   The One without End; Utterly Unknowable; Source of All Being

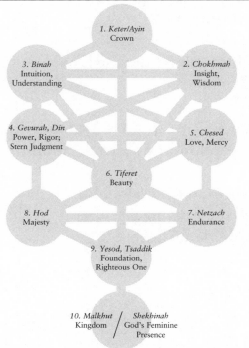

5 All of this is the unfolding of the detailed structure of the lower realms of the pleroma, completing the full realm of God. It is, more than anything else, a psychological diagram of the mind of God so that each being, although apparently a separate entity, is really a separate function within God. In effect, the Secret Book of John anticipates the later construction of the structure of God in the form of the kabbalistic tree of life illustrated above, where ten spheres *(sephiroth)* are carefully organized to show the internal relations behind divine functioning. The diagrams that follow are not the same as the kabbalistic diagram, but they stem from the same desire to show the schematics of divine potential from the top level—*Ayn Sof,* or "the One"—to the lowest level—Malkhut (Kingdom) for the kabbalists and Sophia (Wisdom) for the Gnostics. The Secret Book of John implies a complex three-dimensional mandala structure, as illustrated on page 46.

The third light is called Daveithai and it stands over
   the third realm.
     With Daveithai are
Understanding
Love
Idea.

The fourth light is called Eleleth and it stands over
   the fourth realm.
     With Eleleth are
Perfection
Peace
Wisdom (Sophia).

These are the four lights standing before the Divine
   Autogenes.[5]

(continued on page 47)

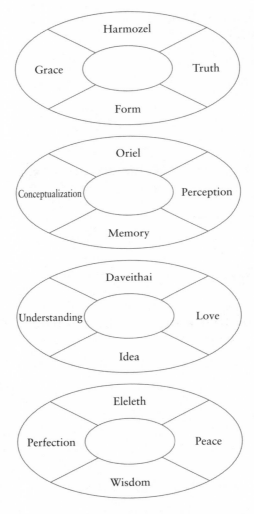

6 You should be sure not to think of these realms, or aeons, as places. Similarly, they are not mythological people, and they are not astrological categories or spaces in a heavenly kingdom. They are aspects of the divine mind.

Twelve realms stand before the Son of the Powerful[6]
   The Autogenes
   The Christ
       Through the intention
       And the grace
   Of the Invisible Spirit
Twelve realms belong to the Son of the Autogenes.

(continued on page 49)

7   The divine mind has unfolded in three separate stages. First, we have heard of the inexpressible conscious One. Then arose the self-awareness of the One, which took form as the Mother, Barbelo, generating a structure in mandala form as discussed earlier. Finally, the coming into being of a form of mental activity called the Son or Christ the Autogenes was revealed. Each stage of the unfolding is more complicated than the last. The present stage has a fourfold structure featuring a series of mandalas. They are not separate entities but aspects of the Son, who is not a person but a set of mental potentials, all of which emerge from the One, here called "the Invisible Spirit." As a whole (a fullness or pleroma) this is the structure of the mind of God.

[All of this came into being through the intention of
   the Holy Spirit
Through the Autogenes.][7]

From the perfect mind's Foreknowledge,
   Through the intention of the Invisible Spirit
   And the Autogenes's will,
The perfect human appeared,
   Its first true manifestation.

(continued on page 51)

8 This is the beginning of the human race in its cosmic and eternal form. There are four separate categories of human and each will be given its own place in the structure of God. We begin with Adamas, who is the perfect ideal of humanity: a realm or "aeon" in the mind of God. The name Adamas is, in one sense, a Greek word meaning "hard" or "invincible"; it is related to the English *adamant* and is at the root of the word *diamond.* In another sense, it comes from the Hebrew *adam,* meaning "mankind." The Adam of Genesis is discussed in detail later in the text.

The Virgin Spirit named the human Adamas[8]
  And placed him over the first realm with the mighty
    autogenes Christ
  With the first light Harmozel and its powers.
The Invisible One gave Adamas invincible power of
  mind.

(continued on page 53)

9 The actions of Adamas are described in the same way as the actions of the other mental functions and abstractions that have come into being: all stand and praise and glorify. But only Adamas speaks words. No previous power has done that; their praises are purely conceptual. The speaking of words here brings us down a level yet again. At the beginning of the story, the infinite inadequacy of words was stressed; now they are being used even in the heavenly realms. Adamas's words are similar to the Gospel of Thomas's saying 77 where Jesus says of himself, "I am the light above everything. I am everything. Everything came forth from me and everything reached to me."

Adamas spoke, glorifying and praising the Invisible
  Spirit:[9]
    "Everything has come into being from you
    Everything will return to you.
    I will praise you and glorify you
        And the Autogenes
        And the triple realm: Father-Mother-Son, the
            perfect power."

(continued on page 55)

10 The "triple realm" (Father-Mother-Son) is the whole of the divine structure described in the Secret Book of John. Jesus introduced himself as Father-Mother-Son in the first pages of the text, and we are now coming to the completion of the divine system of the Son. Adamas and Seth (names derived from Genesis) are central to two of the realms diagramed previously. Note that from the Gnostic perspective Cain and Abel are not part of the divinely originated human race.

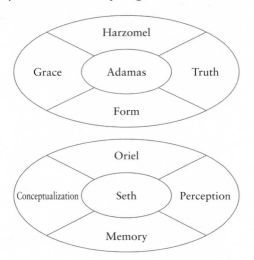

11 Finally, people appear. This concludes the first major section of the Secret Book of John. Thus far, the unfolding and structuring of the mind of God has taken place smoothly: as each higher set of functions comes to completion, a lower set—one more complex but less potent than its predecessors—commences. Everything is in accordance with the divine order. This will change. In the crisis to come, the world begins and, ultimately, comes to an end. Aspects of the Divine appear in the world and are rescued from it; they are referred to here as "the children of Seth" and "the souls of the saints"; earlier they were called "the immovable race." The third and fourth realms described at this point are their final dwelling places: the aeons of those who are saved and who are about to be saved. We are all part of the divine mind from this beginning, as the present section of the story stipulates.

Over the second realm was appointed Adamas's son
    Seth[10]
    With the second light Oriel.

In the third realm were placed the children of Seth,
    With the third light Daveithai.
        [The souls of the saints are placed there.][11]

(continued on page 57)

12 The fourth realm is the dwelling place of those who are not yet saved. Everyone, according to the way of thinking of the Secret Book of John, has divinity within, and that divine power will ultimately be returned to its rightful place. For those who fail to resume their rightful place for a long period, a special lowest place is set aside. This is the fourth realm, the last place of all. And yet it is still a place within God.

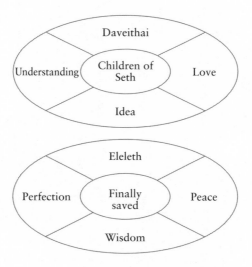

In the fourth realm were placed the souls of those
   ignorant of the fullness
     Those who did not repent at once
     But who, after some time, eventually repented,
     They are with the fourth light Eleleth.[12]

All of these created beings glorify the Invisible Spirit.

1 This passage tells of the crisis in the psychic life of God that leads to the production of the world. The lowest of the divine mental capacities, the realm of Wisdom (*Sophia* in Greek), decides to act independently of the rest of God's mind. Sophia, in an imitation of the self-conscious awareness that the One exhibited at the outset of the development of the divine mind, wishes to think of herself, to see an image of herself. In Gnostic mythology this is the fall; it is not the fall of Adam but the fall of God through God's wisdom. The fall is a false desire for independent objective self-knowledge, the desire to know yourself apart from the whole mind of God. When you are part of the whole mind of God as God's wisdom is, then the impossible quest for objective self-knowledge is a quest for objective knowledge of God, but God is, as you are, entirely subjective.

2 The whole of the unfolding universe of aeons constituting the mind of God is a single complex entity. For one element of that whole entity to seek itself individually apart from the whole—the pleroma—is to seek something that is contrary to divine nature. Part of a harmonious mind cannot act independently of the whole mind without insanity ensuing. And insanity does begin here. Although the Secret Book of John does not use this language, it appears to be the case that God has gone mad or, to put it less strongly, an aspect of the mind of God has malfunctioned. The rest of the book tells the consequences of this malfunction and of the efforts to repair the system. Divine madness receives psychotherapy that is the history of the world.

☐ A Crisis That Became the World

It happened that the realm (aeon) Wisdom (Sophia)
 Of conceptual thought (Epinoia),
 Began to think for herself,[1]
  She used the thinking (enthymesis)
  And the foreknowledge (prognosis)
  Of the Invisible Spirit.

She intended to reveal an image from herself
 To do so without the consent of the Spirit,
  Who did not approve,[2]
 Without the thoughtful assistance of her masculine
  counterpart,
  Who did not approve.

(continued on page 61)

3   In the Hebrew Bible's book of Proverbs, especially in chapters 1 and 8, God's wisdom is sometimes treated as an entity independent of God, which in that context is only a literary device, not a theological principle. But it appeared to some people to be a theological principle, for Wisdom speaks, she travels down to this world to be received sometimes and rejected most of the time, and she assists God in creation. The idea of an independently acting Wisdom may have seemed a problematic notion to the Gnostics. They developed the idea that Wisdom wrongly acted independently of God and, therefore, she fell into crisis.

❖   The wisdom of God never stops being part of the mind of God. Accordingly, even though Sophia (Wisdom) misconceives herself and thinks in an improper manner not in accord with the rest of the divine mind, her thoughts take place nonetheless. What takes place in the mind of God is reality. Accordingly, because Sophia retains divine power, her thoughts become reality. The fact that a reality is sustained by this divine power means that if divine power is withdrawn, that reality will cease to exist. Sophia's power is what sustains our world. Its withdrawal is God's providential plan to ensure that all divine power will forever attain and remain in the fullness of God.

4   The idea of God's wisdom, Sophia, having creative power is attested in the canonical book of Proverbs in the Hebrew Bible, where she is present with God during creation as a semi-independent aspect of God (8:22–36). In Proverbs her role is entirely positive, but the idea of God's wisdom being active in creation led, eventually, to the Gnostic interpretation of Wisdom's creative role as being a disastrous mistake.

Without the Invisible Spirit's consent
  Without the knowledge of her partner
    She brought it into being.[3]

Because she had unconquerable power
Her thought was not unproductive.
  Something imperfect came out of her[4]
  Different in appearance from her.

(continued on page 63)

5 Although the Secret Book of John does not give us the details, it presupposes that each feminine-named aspect of the divine mind has a corresponding masculine-named aspect. Hence, we heard earlier of a set of five aeons being, really, a set of ten androgynous aeons. Sophia's masculine-named counterpart is mentioned here, but we are never told his name. The thought of the wisdom of God, in isolation from her counterpart, produces a monstrous virgin birth.

6 Instead of the self-awareness that she had tried to attain—an awareness that is impossible for an aspect of the divine mind—Sophia conceives of something that is incoherent. In physical terms, it is misshapen. In the ancient world, it was often believed that in the production of an infant the male provided form and the female substance. In the absence of the male element, Sophia has produced only substance.

7 After its initial emergence as a misshapen mass, Sophia's inadequate and mistaken self-image takes on monstrous form. As it cannot persist in the realm of the divine mind, where Sophia properly belongs, she casts it out of that realm. In so doing she begins the process that brings our world into being. If hell is defined as being "without God," then Sophia has just created hell and thrown her product into it.

8 Material existence is beginning here. Instead of hearing only about powers emerging and praising and glorifying, now we have a creature with a physical appearance, and a throne amidst clouds. Sophia's intention is for him to be alone, drifting and hidden. But he has taken power from her; he is a mental mistake by God's wisdom, and so he himself has something of the creative power that is inherent in God's mind.

9 Like the name Barbelo, the name Yaldabaoth has been the subject of much scholarly speculation. Some have suggested that it comes from phrases in Hebrew or Aramaic such as "son of chaos," "begetter of heavens," or "god of desires," but there is no agreement on the subject, and most of the suggestions don't fit very well with Yaldabaoth's role in the myth. As with the name Barbelo, it is probably best to take Yaldabaoth as simply a name, not associated with a specific meaning.

Because she had created it without her masculine counterpart[5]
　She gave rise to a misshapen being unlike herself.[6]

Sophia saw what her desire produced.
　It changed into the form of a dragon with a lion's head
　And eyes flashing lightning bolts.
She cast him far from her,
　Outside of the realm of the immortal beings
　So that they could not see him.[7]
[She had created him in ignorance.]

Sophia surrounded him with a brilliant cloud,
　Put a throne in the center part of the cloud,[8]
　So that no one would see it.
　[Except for the Holy Spirit called the Mother of the Living.]
She named him Yaldabaoth.[9]

(continued on page 65)

10 He is called ruler, which is *archon* in Greek. His subordinates will also be called archons or *exousia*—"power" or "energy"—and sometimes even called his angels. But in English, the word *demon* describes them all best. They may be imagined to rule subordinate spaces in the created world, spaces inadequately and incompetently modeled on the realms above. In the *Timaeus,* Plato wrote about a god-craftsman called the demiurge who constructed this created world based on ideal forms he observed in the higher realm. Plato's demiurge does a good job, although hampered by the imperfections of matter, and is a positively valued being. Yaldabaoth is a deliberate perversion of this demiurge idea, a bad craftsman basing his world on misunderstood, dimly seen models in the higher realm. In a sense, the Gnostics seem to have thought that Plato misunderstood Platonism, valuing a demiurge who should not be admired or valued. Similarly, as we shall see, the Gnostics thought that Moses had misunderstood the foundational Genesis myth of Judaism.

11 Since Yaldabaoth has something of the creative power of God's wisdom, which itself stems from the Invisible Spirit, Yaldabaoth can imagine things into being. His thoughts become realities just as Sophia's did. Human thoughts too will become realities; either negative passions or divine spiritual intuitions will dominate, depending on the person who is thinking. Since reality only consists of the realms of God, Yaldabaoth imagines such realms for himself: artificial imitations of the real, aeons existing in a new space that is removed from the divine. Yaldabaoth's moving, first because his mother drove him away and now on his own volition, is the creation of space itself.

Yaldabaoth is the chief ruler.[10]
>He took great power (dynamis) from his mother,
>>Left her and moved away from his birthplace.
>He assumed command,
>>Created realms for himself[11]
>With a brilliant flame that continues to exist even
>now.

1 In a parody of Sophia's failure to join with her masculine counterpart, here Yaldabaoth mates with his partner, thoughtlessness, to engender ruling powers for his lower world. They are the gods of this world.

2 The names of the rulers of the seven heavens are sometimes understandable: Athoth is Thoth, Egyptian god of wisdom; Harmas is Hermes, the Greek god associated with Thoth in Hermetic literature; Kalilaoumbri is of unknown origin; the origin of Yabel is also unknown, although it might be ultimately derived from the word *Yahweh* combined with the word *baal,* which means "Lord" in Hebrew; Adonai Sabaoth means "Lord of Hosts," a common Jewish phrase for God; and Cain and Abel are the sons of Adam from Genesis. All of these beings, from the Gnostic perspective, are false gods entrapping humans below who properly should ascend to resume their status as elements in the mind of God. The names of the rulers of the five lower spheres are obscure. Melcheir-adonein may mean "King Lord" and Belias probably is a variant of Belial the demon's name. Divine and demonic names used in texts like the Secret Book of John often vary in their spellings from one usage to the next. For example, the name for the ruler of the fifth realm is here spelled Adonai Sabaoth, but elsewhere is spelled Adonein Sabaoth or even just Adonin. This happens because of scribal errors that accumulate over the centuries.

□ The Fashioning of This World

Yaldabaoth united with the thoughtlessness (aponoia)
   within him.[1]
He begot ruling authorities (exousia)
   Modeling them on the incorruptible realms above.

The first is Athoth
The second is Harmas [called the eye of flame]
The third is Kalilaoumbri
The fourth is Yabel
The fifth is Adonai [called Sabaoth]
The sixth is Cain [called the sun]
The seventh is Abel

The eighth is Abrisene
The ninth is Yobel
The tenth is Armupiel
The eleventh is Melcheir-adonein
The twelfth is Belias[2]
   Who rules over the very depth of Hades.

(continued on page 69)

3 The geometry of reality has changed. We no longer find an expansive mandala structure here, but an imprisoning and claustrophobic series of concentric spheres rising above and descending below the world. The first seven spheres contain the mobile celestial beings: the five visible planets (Mercury, Venus, Mars, Jupiter, and Saturn), the sun, and the moon. Note that these planets retain the names, in English, of the Roman gods who were thought to rule there. In the series of concentric spheres, the surface of the earth is beneath the seventh sphere, Abel, which probably corresponds with the location of the moon. Immediately above it is Cain, corresponding with the location of the sun. Beneath the surface of the earth are five additional spheres culminating in the one ruled over by Belias in the furthest reaches of Hades (in Coptic, literally *amente,* the Egyptian underworld).

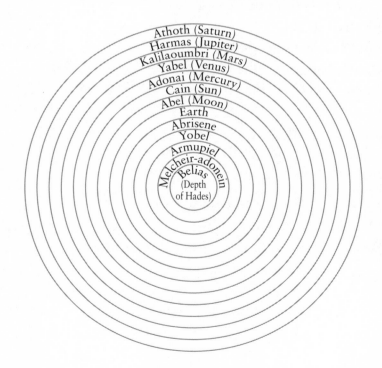

Athoth (Saturn)
Harmas (Jupiter)
Kalilaoumbri (Mars)
Yabel (Venus)
Adonai (Mercury)
Cain (Sun)
Abel (Moon)
Earth
Abrisene
Yobel
Armupiel
Melcheir-adonein
Belias
(Depth of Hades)

He made the first seven rulers to reign in the seven
   spheres of heaven.
He made the next five rulers to reign in the five depths
   of the abyss.[3]

(continued on page 71)

4 The Secret Book of John differentiates between Yaldabaoth's fire, which is his own nature, and his light, which is the power he receives from his mother. His power is his "genetic inheritance" going back to Sophia, and from her back to Christ the Son, within whose system of realms she came into being, and from Christ the Son back to the Invisible Spirit from whom all blessings flow. As the thoughts of God are part of the mind of God, and therefore all are real, and as Yaldabaoth is a mistaken thought, his existence is sustained by that power. But his fire is his own and is ultimately unreal; he can share it with his subordinates. If Yaldabaoth's power can be taken from him and returned to the world of the divine mind, his fire will go out and his world will come to an end. Here the power of the mind of God that brought Yaldabaoth into existence and that sustains him is called light. The nature of the whole lower realm now coming into being is the opposite: darkness. And yet the darkness only exists through the sustaining power of the light. The author of the Secret Book of John is trying to depict a reality where the lower realm is neither light nor darkness but a gloomy mixture of the two.

5 *Saklas* is Aramaic for "fool" and was applied to Satan in Judaism. *Samael* means "blind god" in Aramaic. These terms are used in other Gnostic texts for Yaldabaoth and so here, as elsewhere, the author of the Secret Book of John acknowledges that there are alternative versions of the story he is telling.

6 Here we have a clear reflection of influence from the Jewish biblical tradition: a quotation from Isaiah 46:9, "I am God, and there is no God but me!" In the context of the Secret Book of John this is absurd, a testimony to Yaldabaoth's ignorance and arrogance. Of course there is a higher God than he; we heard about it at great length in the first section of this book. Yaldabaoth owes his existence to that higher God and should know about him. But he doesn't. The equation of the Divine Being who speaks in the Isaiah prophecy with Yaldabaoth himself foreshadows the equation of Yaldabaoth with the creator god of Genesis.

He shared a portion of his fire with them,
   But shared none of the power of light he had
      received from his mother.[4]
   [He is ignorant darkness.
When the light mingled into the darkness, the darkness
   shone.
When darkness mixed with the light, the light
   diminished,
   No longer light nor darkness but dim.]

This dim ruler has three names:
   Yaldabaoth is the first.
   Saklas is the second.
   Samael is the third.[5]
He is blasphemous through his thoughtlessness.
He said "I am God, and there is no God but me!"
   Since he didn't know where his own power
      originated.[6]

(continued on page 73)

7 The creation of the lower world continues. One should imagine this developing cosmos as a more temporal than a spatial construction. Yaldabaoth creates the times and seasons that govern life: first, the astrological forces, which are the twelve authorities discussed in the previous sequence; and second, the mundane daily forces, which are discussed here. The seven authorities created here are the days of the week, each of which is ruled by a particular demonic power. In *Apocryphon Johannis,* Giversen suggests that the Secret Book of John tells us of three names for Yaldabaoth, twelve spheres with ruling authorities, seven demonic rulers with seven authorities each who, in turn, have six demons each, giving us a grand total of $3 + 12 + 7 + (7 \times 7) + (49 \times 6) = 365$. Every day has its own demon. The magicians and physicians of the ancient world knew their names, when they had greatest influence, and what should be done about them. The Secret Book of John is telling us these odd names for practical reasons. Note that our English words for the days of the week reflect the idea that specific gods rule the various days. In our case, most of them are Norse gods: Tiu rules Tuesday, Woden rules Wednesday, Thor rules Thursday, Freya rules Friday.

8 Some of the names of these demons are similar to the names of those who rule the astrological spheres. Athoth is the same, Eloaios may derive from *Elohim,* and Yao stems from *Yahweh,* both of which are Jewish names for God. Adonein Sabaoth has here been divided into "hosts" and "lord" separately in the fifth and sixth position. Sabbataios, the seventh, comes from *Sabbath.* Why they have the faces they are said to have is unknown, although the idea of animal-headed ruling authorities probably stems from ancient Egypt. Isaiah 6:2 tells us that the seraphim kept their faces hidden with their wings. Here we evidently find out why they did that. The separation of various Jewish names for the one God into individual names for separate supernatural beings is a common characteristic of ancient magical practice.

His rulers created seven authorities for themselves.
  Each of these authorities created six demons apiece,
  There came to be 365 demons altogether.[7]

Here are the seven authorities' names and physical
  forms:
  First, Athoth with a sheep's face
  Second, Eloaios with a donkey's face
  Third, Astaphaios with a hyena's face
  Fourth, Yao with the face of a seven-headed snake
  Fifth, Sabaoth who has the face of a dragon
  Sixth, Adonin whose face is that of a monkey
  Seventh, Sabbataios with a face of flame and fire.[8]
These are the seven of the week.
These authorities rule the world.

Yaldabaoth has many faces,
  More than all that have been listed
  So he can convey any face he wants to the seraphim
    around him.

(continued on page 75)

9 Yaldabaoth remains an order of magnitude superior to his demonic assistants, here called seraphim. In the Gnostic view, the seraphim of the biblical God are actually the demons of Yaldabaoth. They have specific powers and faces; he has all powers and all faces, and each of their separate faces is a reflection of one of Yaldabaoth's faces. We hear again that Yaldabaoth's light from his divine origin through God's wisdom is his alone; up to now his subordinates have been given only the infinitely inferior fire.

10 Yaldabaoth's willingness to mingle his power from his mother's light with his own dark fire was discussed earlier. Now he conjoins seven forms of the power from the realm of light with seven fire-possessing, demonic authorities of his own creation. The divine elements of Goodness, Forethought, and so forth are indeed entailed in his own power, for his power derives only from the higher realm and so Yaldabaoth has positive potentials within himself. It is part of the divine plan, Providence, to undermine Yaldabaoth's demons by conjoining them with divine elements that will destroy them. Evidently the power within Yaldabaoth is capable of acting on its own and causing Yaldabaoth to act against his own interests. The realms of beneficent divine powers that are paired up with Yaldabaoth's demonic forces will ultimately undermine his constructed reality and enable everything divine to return to the world of the One. Yaldabaoth has planted the seed of his own destruction. As it turns out, not only does each day have its demon, but each day has also a force for good associated with it, as illustrated on page 76.

Yaldabaoth shared his fire with his seraphim
   But gave them none of his pure light
   Although he ruled them by virtue of the power and
     glory
      Of the light he had received from his mother.[9]
   [Therefore he called himself God and defied his
     place of origin.]

He united his thought's sevenfold powers with the
   authorities who accompanied him.
   He spoke and it happened.
He named those sevenfold powers starting with the
   highest one:
   Goodness paired with the first: Athoth
   Providence paired with the second: Eloaios
   Divinity paired with the third: Astaphaios
   Lordship paired with the fourth: Yao
   Kingdom paired with the fifth: Sabaoth
   Zeal paired with the sixth: Adonin
   Understanding paired with the seventh:
     Sabbataios.[10]

(continued on page 77)

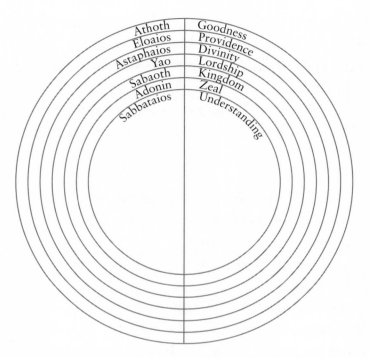

Athoth
Eloaios
Astaphaios
Yao
Sabaoth
Adonin
Sabbataios

Goodness
Providence
Divinity
Lordship
Kingdom
Zeal
Understanding

See p. 72 for discussion of the origin of these demons' names.

11 Yaldabaoth models his lower creation on an inadequately known and dimly visible higher divine world. This is a Platonic view of things: A demiurge god manufactures a world, modeling it on the realm of perfect ideas. This demiurge, though, knows barely anything of the perfect world it is trying to copy. Now it is suddenly motivated to produce a system of realms that are component parts of the higher divine world. What seems to be happening here is that the power of the mind of God that brought Yaldabaoth into being is not an unconscious energy but an active conscious actor in this cosmic drama. Power is trapped within Yaldabaoth and is unable, thus far, to escape. But power has

(continued on page 78)

Each has its own realm modeled on one of the higher
   realms,
      And each new name refers to a glory in the heavens
      So that Yaldabaoth's demons might be destroyed.
The demons' own names, given by Yaldabaoth, are
   mighty names
But the powers' names reflecting the glory above
      Will bring about the demons' destruction and
         remove their power.
         That is why each has two names.

Yaldabaoth modeled his creation on the pattern of the
   original realms above him
So that it might be just like the indestructible realms.

   [Not that he had ever seen the indestructible ones.
   Rather, the power in him deriving from his mother
   Made him aware of the pattern of the cosmos
      above.][11]

(continued on page 79)

caused Yaldabaoth to bring into being the parallel realms of Goodness, Providence, Divinity, and so forth. It now partially reveals to him the structures of the realm above, the mind of God. As Yaldabaoth works to imitate that world he will ultimately bring about his own destruction.

12 Yaldabaoth's declaration, "I am a jealous God and there is no God but me," comes from Exodus 20:3–5, the beginning of the Ten Commandments. From the perspective of the Secret Book of John, this is Yaldabaoth bragging about his predominance. In the context of the present text he is speaking nonsense, for he is a hugely subordinate and incompetent fragment of the true God.

❖ This concludes the third major section of the Secret Book of John. First we heard of the Incomprehensible One, and then of the development of the mind of God, the pleroma, the highest realm of aeons. Third came the narrative of the fall of Sophia, her production of Yaldabaoth, and his subsequent creation of a series of concentric lower realms and demonic servants modeled incompetently on the higher world. Next we will hear of the beginning of the restoration of Yaldabaoth's power back to the higher world and the eventual end of the world he brought into being, a process that begins with the creation of human beings.

When he gazed upon his creation surrounding him
   He said to his host of demons
   The ones who had come forth out of him:
"I am a jealous God and there is no God but me!"[12]

   [But by doing this he admitted to his demons that
      there is indeed another God.
   For if there were no other God, who would he
      possibly be jealous of?]

1 The movement of Yaldabaoth's mother, Sophia, the wisdom of God, contrasts with the standing and stability and immovable nature of the upper world. Her movement signifies her involvement in the realm of matter and darkness. Her divine power is, metaphorically, light. Some power, or light, has gone into Yaldabaoth, enabling his structuring of an incompetent world modeled on the higher world, and accordingly, her share is lessened, or dimmed.

2 Suddenly, for the first time since the early pages of the text, we are reminded that the literary structure of the Secret Book of John is a dialogue between John and the revealed ascended Jesus. John asks about Genesis 1:2 where the Spirit moves over the primordial waters. It was assumed then (and often still is assumed) that Moses wrote the book of Genesis. From the viewpoint of the Secret Book of John, the basic story in Genesis is true, that myth is valid, but the version of it written down by Moses is incorrect. The Secret Book of John is, in part, a corrective to Moses's version of the Genesis creation story, giving us the true version according to the Gnostics.

3 Sophia's motion, in contrast with divine stability, indicates her fallen state and her awareness of her fallen state, which translates into the desire to repair that state, beginning with her repentance. As she is not able to return to the realm above, because a portion of her divine power is in Yaldabaoth, and yet she is alien to Yaldabaoth's realm below, she vacillates between the two—that is her movement.

□ Sophia Repents

His mother began to move back and forth
    Because she had become aware that she now lacked
        light
    For her brightness had dimmed.[1]
    [Since her consort had not approved of her actions
        She grew darker]

I said "Master, what does it mean 'she moved back and
    forth'?"
He laughed, saying, "It's not as Moses said 'upon the
    waters.' Not at all.[2]

When she saw the evil that had taken place and
    The theft of light that her son had committed
She repented.

In the darkness of ignorance
    She began to forget.
    She began to be ashamed.
        But she could not yet return above
        Yet she began to move.
And so she moved back and forth."[3]

(continued on page 83)

❖ This redundant summary probably was added by someone who usually followed a different version of the Secret Book of John. The scribal addition of summaries here and there in the text shows that, just like most modern readers, ancient readers found this narrative hard to follow. This summary describes the "weeping" of Sophia rather than her "movement." The ideas amount to the same thing, both signifying the beginning of the effort to undo what Yaldabaoth has done. The first stage of that undoing is, necessarily, awareness of the problem. In these passages, Sophia has become aware of the consequences of her mistake. Yaldabaoth is a metaphorical miscarriage, with substance (from the Mother) but no form (from the Father).

4 The pleroma, the fullness or the complete mind of God, hears Wisdom's repentance and asks for assistance from the Father, the Invisible or Virgin Spirit, who pours out his Spirit on her as it was poured out upon the Son earlier in the text. This begins the process of salvation and models it for all those human beings who will follow. As humans realize their unhappy situation and repent, they too can expect the Spirit to be poured out upon them. Note that the process Sophia did *not* follow (leading to her fall) is now being followed properly; the whole mind of God works together instead of one function operating separately.

5 Logically enough, we hear that Wisdom's error cannot be repaired by her masculine-named counterpart acting alone. It was acting alone that got her into trouble in the first place, so more acting alone will not save her. Rather, the whole of the mind of God acting in a harmonious system will now begin her rescue and restoration.

[The arrogant one removed power from his mother
    For he was ignorant
    He thought no one existed except for his mother.
He saw the host of demons he had created
    And he elevated himself above them.
But when his mother realized that that miscarriage
    Was so imperfect
      She came to realize that her consort had not
        approved.
She repented and wept furiously.]

All of the divine realms (pleroma) heard her repentant
    prayer;
They sought blessing for her from the Invisible Virgin
    Spirit.
    The Spirit consented.
    He poured the Holy Spirit over her
        Brought forth from the whole full realm.[4]

[Her consort did not come down to her on his own,
but he came through the whole full realm
to restore her to her original condition.][5]

(continued on page 85)

6   The full restoration of the lost power of God, his fallen Wisdom, will take place when humans have ascended to the higher realm. So long as there are people within this lower world (you and I, for example), Sophia will have to wait. The ninth sphere has to do with the ancient astrological vision of the universe as having seven fundamental spheres of the sun, the moon, and the five visible planets surmounted by an eighth sphere for the fixed stars. Beyond that, the realm of the Divine was thought to begin. Thus, the ninth sphere would be the very lowest part of that realm: an interface between this world and the divine world. The eighth sphere is, therefore, the sphere of Yaldabaoth, below which come the seven spheres beginning with Athoth's and descending from there.

She was elevated above her son,
　　But she was not restored to her own original realm.
She would remain in the ninth sphere until she was
　　fully restored.[6]

1 We know, but Yaldabaoth does not, that Providence (Pronoia, Barbelo, Mother) with permission of the Father is the source of the image of the First Man. "The Man exists" refers to Barbelo, who was called First Man (and Thrice Male, etc.). Bear in mind that the sexual designations for divine functions are not to be taken seriously. The "Son of Man" refers to the Son, or Christ, the final unfolding of the divine mind. The Secret Book of John reveals that the image of God, the human image shone forth to Yaldabaoth, is the whole fullness, the entire pleroma, the Father and the Mother and the Son.

2 The rescue of Sophia's divine power begins. The whole realm of the divine mind, the pleroma, described in detail earlier, now is manifested to Yaldabaoth in a special form. The power within him has previously revealed to him, in a dim and inadequate manner, the nature of the realm above and he has made an incompetent effort to reproduce it in the form of the lower world, an activity that is a continuation of Wisdom's self-contradictory effort to apprehend the whole of the pleroma by herself. Here, for the first time, the whole pleroma, the divine mind and image of God, ultimate reality, clearly shines forth not in mandala form but in the form of a perfect human being.

3 Divine revelation destabilizes the very structure of lower reality. At the outset of the Secret Book of John, the world quaked when Jesus first revealed his ascended presence to John. Here the revelation of the image of God, Man and the Son of Man (who are not two different beings but two structures within the full pleroma of the divine mind), begins the process that will remove this world from being. We will again hear of the quaking of the foundations in the Secret Book of John's concluding hymn.

☐ Humanity Begins

Then came a voice from the highest realms saying:
    "The Man exists! And the Son of Man!"
Yaldabaoth, chief ruler, heard it,
    He thought it came from his Mother,
    He did not know the true source of the voice:
        The Holy Mother-Father
        Perfect Providence
        Image of the Invisible
            Father of Everything
            In whom everything has come to be.[1]

The First Man
    This is the one who appeared to them.
    He appeared in the form of a human being.[2]

All of the realm of the chief ruler quaked!
    The foundations of the abyss moved![3]

(continued on page 89)

4   As does the Hebrew Bible in Genesis 1:6–8, the Secret Book of John assumes that above the sky is water and below the earth is water. If you look up beyond the stars into the blackness of night, what you see is water. This heavenly realm of water is the ninth sphere, the temporary abode of Sophia. Normally it is dark in the spaces beyond the stars; now, suddenly, it is illuminated. We already heard that the whole fullness was revealed to Sophia in the ninth sphere, now we hear about the form that fullness takes when apprehended from below: the form of a human being.

5   The rulers and especially Yaldabaoth see the image of God, the prototypical human being, reflected in the waters above the earth, surrounded and illuminated by supernal light. This is part of the Secret Book of John's ongoing revision of Moses's account in Genesis; this passage is the true story behind the idea of mankind being made in the image of God.

6   In this sequence, the myth returns to the very beginning of the story. The One gazed into its own light and saw itself reflected there. The self that was seen came into being as Barbelo and the whole unfolding of the divine mind followed. Now that divine mind is reflected in light above this world and the construction of humanity will follow based on that reflection of a reflection.

7   This is a reworking of the Genesis creation myth. The Secret Book of John accepts its structure but believes the standard interpretation of the myth—that of Moses—is in error. Here Genesis 1:27 is at issue: "Let us make man in our image, after our likeness." Yaldabaoth will eventually end up with a man that is, in some respects, like the Image he has seen ("in our image") and, in other respects, like the beings of his lower world ("after our likeness"). Since their world is so dim, Yaldabaoth and his demons hope to retain some of the illumination that emblazoned the Divine Image in the waters above.

He illuminated the waters above the world of matter,
    His image shown in those waters.[4]

All the demons and the first ruler together gazed up
    Toward the underside of the newly shining waters.[5]
Through that light they saw the Image in the waters.[6]

Yaldabaoth said to his subordinate demons:
    "Let's create a man according to the image of God
        And our own likeness
    So that his image will illuminate us!"[7]

(continued on page 91)

8　Yaldabaoth acts through the subordinate demons that he has previously brought into being. Each power creates an aspect of the first human being, a process that will be detailed as the story unfolds. At this stage of Adam's creation, each demon works through an associated power, as will be elaborated in the next section.

9　Because the demonic powers know about Adam from the illuminated vision they had of him in the waters above, they expect that when they have completed his creation, he will help illuminate their dim world. Ironically, he will eventually remove from their world all of the light power that it now contains.

Each one through another's power created aspects of
   the man;
      Each added a characteristic corresponding to the
         psychic factors
      They had seen in the Image above them.[8]
They made a creature of substance
In the likeness of that perfect First Man
And they said, "Let us call him Adam, so that his name
   will give us the power of light."[9]

❖ As Yaldabaoth created his demonic subordinates through the divine power he received from his mother, God's wisdom, he could not help but allow divine aspects of the power to affiliate with those demons. Astaphaios with a hyena's face had Divinity associated with it; Lordship came to Yao, whose face was that of a seven-headed serpent; and so forth. Now those divine powers take action in the process of creating the human "image of God." They work from the inside out, from the physically deepest part of the human body, the bones, toward the surface features of skin and hair. But this is a human made out of psyche by divine powers; matter is not yet involved. The term *psyche* has to do with a person's conscious self or animating element. It means "soul" and implies the presence of consciousness and divinity.

1 From here on out, demons will be controlling the creation process until the material body is completed, but at the outset, humanity is soul or psyche only. The body parts and factors are ideal forms rather than the material parts they eventually will be. While Gnostics generally thought that the physical human body was a dwelling place of demons and an imprisonment for the divine power humans will eventually possess, this part of the Secret Book of John implies that our underlying physical structure is not without divine inspiration. A human being is modeled on the revealed full mind of God, the pleroma. The various forms of psyche—souls or animations of the various features of the human body—are brought about through the work of the divine powers within Yaldabaoth's demonic underworld. We will hear shortly about the demons' creation of an imprisoning material body to encase the psychic body. Paul writes about the two types of body in 1 Corinthians 15:50–54, but in his view the immaterial body will replace the material body; according to the Secret Book of John, the two bodies now coexist in every person.

☐ The Construction of the Human Body

The seven Powers began to work:
 Goodness made a psyche of bone
 Providence made a psyche of sinew
 Divinity made a psyche of flesh
 Lordship made a psyche of marrow
 Kingdom made a psyche of blood
 Zeal made a psyche of skin
 Understanding made a psyche of hair.[1]

The host of demons took these substances from the powers to create the limbs and the body itself. They put the parts together and coordinated them.

The first ones began by making the head:
Abron created his head; Meniggesstroeth created the brain; Asterechme, the right eye; Thaspomocha, the left eye; Ieronumos, the right ear; Bissoum, the left ear; Akioreim, the nose; Banenrphroum, the lips; Amen, the front teeth; Ibikan, the molars; Basiliademe, the tonsils;

(continued on page 95)

2   The reason we are hearing the exact names of each demon who created and continues to supervise each part of the body is because this is crucial knowledge in the medical system that provided care for most of the people in the ancient world: magic. Exorcists and magicians were the physicians of the day; Jesus of Nazareth was one of them. One of the primary requisites for curing physical ailments was to know the names of the demons controlling the affected parts of the body so that they could be propitiated or exorcised—bought off or driven out. Without knowing their names, and usually their names were secret knowledge, one could not hope to control them. This complex list of names empowers magicians and exorcists to cure. The Testament of Solomon (available on the Internet) is an example of an ancient Jewish exorcist's medical manual.

❖   This material, and the following few pages, are absent in the short version of the Secret Book of John.

tonsils; Achcha, the uvula; Adaban, the neck;
Chaaman, the neckbones; Dearcho, the throat; Tebar,
the shoulder; Mniarcon, the elbow; Abitrion, the right
arm; Evanthen, the left arm; Krys, the right hand;
Beluai, the left hand; Treneu, the fingers of the right
hand; Balbel, the fingers of the left hand; Kriman,
fingernails; Astrops, the right breast; Barroph, the left
breast; Baoum, the right shoulder joint; Ararim, the left
shoulder joint; Areche, the belly; Phthave, the navel;
Senaphim, the abdomen; Arachethopi, the right ribs;
Zabedo, the left ribs; Barias, the right hip; Phnouth the
left hip; Abenlenarchei, the marrow; Chnoumeninorin,
the skeleton; Gesole, the stomach; Agromauna, the
heart; Bano, the lungs; Sostrapal, the liver; Anesimalar,
the spleen; Thopithro, the intestines; Biblo, the
kidneys; Roeror, the sinews; Taphreo, the spine;
Ipouspoboba, the veins; Bineborin, the arteries;
Atoimenpsephei, respiration; Entholleia, the flesh;
Bedouk, the right buttock; Arabeei, the penis; Eilo, the
testicles; Sorma, the genitals; Gormakaiochlabar, the
right thigh; Nebrith, the left thigh; Pserem, the kidneys
of the right leg; Asaklas, the left kidney; Ormaoth, the
right leg; Emenun, the left leg; Knyx, the right shin;
Tupelon, the left shin; Achiel, the right knee; Phnene,
the left knee; Phiouthrom, the right foot; Boabel, its
toes; Trachoun, the left foot; Phikna, its toes; Miamai,
the toenails.[2]

(continued on page 97)

3 These are the first beings Yaldabaoth created (although their names are spelled a bit differently here than previously). They are equivalent to the astrologically active planetary forces: Saturn, Jupiter, Mars, Venus, Mercury, Sun, and Moon. In accordance with the ancient view of the nature of human life, these demons control the physical elements of the human beings who are coming into existence. We heard previously of seven divine powers bringing into being a psychic framework for the human body. And even further back we heard of those seven powers affiliating themselves with the seven demons of the days of the week. In the present passage, humanity is being taken from its initial, purely psychic form toward a physical form, and the demonic powers are asserting themselves to control it.

4 This sequence largely repeats the body parts listed previously, but the names of the demons are different. The previous list, because it specified "Arabeei, the penis; Eilo, the testicles" is for males, and this list, including "the womb, Sabalo" is for females. Both lists begin at the head, systematically proceed down the torso, and finally end at the toes. The origins of these demonic names are unknown. Possibly, they emerged during the process of exorcisms, when the demons would be interrogated and asked their names. Imagine an ancient magical book with a drawing of a human torso and dozens of lines drawn to various body parts, each connected to the name of the demon to be invoked, or exorcised, in cases of medical necessity.

And those who were appointed over all of these are:
Zathoth,
Armas,
Kalila,
Iabel,
Sabaoth,
Cain,
Abel.[3]

The energizing powers in the limbs were divided among:
the head made by Diolimodraza; the neck by Yammeax; the right shoulder, Yakouib; the left shoulder, Verton; the right hand, Oudidi; the left, Arbao; the fingers of the right hand, Lampno; the fingers of the left hand, Leekaphar; the right breast, Barbar; the left breast, Imae; the chest, Pisandriaptes; the right shoulder joint, Koade; the left shoulder joint, Odeor; the right ribs, Asphixix; the left ribs, Synogchouta; the abdomen, Arouph; the womb, Sabalo; the right thigh, Charcharb; the left thigh, Chthaon; the genitals, Bathinoth; the right leg, Choux; the left leg, Charcha; the right shin, Aroer; the left shin, Toechtha; the right knee, Aol; the left knee, Charaner; the right foot, Bastan; its toes, Archentechtha; the left foot, Marephnounth; its toes, Abrana.[4]

(continued on page 99)

❖ The author of the Secret Book of John has a very dim view of the human body; as presented, it is a hive of demons. Every part, every function, every aspect of the body, even the psychological functions of the body such as the senses and the ability to act, have demonic powers supervising them. Like the list of demons governing each part of the body, this list would have helped ancient exorcists and healers interact with relevant demons by name so they could try to rectify physical and psychological symptoms.

5 The sequence of five governing factors may trace psychological events from their inception to their final outcome. The process seems to begin with direct perception, move to receiving information from the senses, then to imagining the information's form and nature, to integrating that information into the whole mind, and finally to emerge as action of one sort or another. But there is not very much to go on here.

6 The creation of the human body in the Secret Book of John has proceeded from the most abstract elements where powers for good seem to underlie various essential psychic or soul functions: "Goodness made a psyche of bone, Providence made a psyche of sinew," and so forth; through the creation of each physical part and its accompanying demon; down to the fundamental elements that compose the body; and, finally, to the base and the mother of all of this: matter itself.

Seven govern the whole body:
    Michael,
    Ouriel,
    Asmenedas,
    Saphasatoel,
    Aarmouriam,
    Richram,
    Amiorps.

The one who governs perceptions: Archendekta
The one who governs reception: Deitharbathas
The one who governs imagination: Oummaa
The one who governs integration: Aachiaram
The one who governs impulse: Riaramnacho.[5]

There are fourfold sources of the bodily demons: hot,
    cold, dry, wet.
    [Matter is the mother of them all.]
        Ruler of hot: Phloxopha
        Ruler of cold: Oroorrothos
        Ruler of dry: Erimacho
        Ruler of wet: Athuro.

Their mother stands among them: Onorthochrasaei
    She is unlimited
    She mixes with all of them.
    She is matter[6]
        And they are nourished by her.

(continued on page 101)

7 Human beings experience many disagreeable emotions and impulses. In the psychology offered here, these emotions and impulses are caused by factors external to persons themselves. For example, to follow a sequence, shame is a subcategory of the passion fear. Fear emerges from the demonic ruling power Blaomen. Envy stems from the passion called distress, and distress emerges from the demonic Nenentophni. The demons, in turn, arise from their mother Esthesis-Zouch-Epi-Ptoe, a Greek Stoic phrase that Bentley Layton identifies as *aesthesis ouch epi ptoah* or "perception not in a state of excitement."

8 The psychological theory of the Secret Book of John is that demonic powers working through human passions give rise to negative emotions and impulses. This too is a primitive medical theory and not just speculation for its own sake. It arises from the fact that people feel they should have complete control over their emotions and yet, of course, such control takes tremendous work through meditation and ascetic training. So most people find themselves feeling assaulted by passions and emotions that they would choose not to have. Some people in the ancient world concluded that if we do not have complete control of ourselves and our feelings, it follows that our feelings, or passions, are put into us by demonic beings. From the perspective of the Secret Book of John, the demons are thrusting these passions and undesirable feelings and motivations into us as part of their ongoing effort to render us ignorant and forgetful and entrapped.

The four chief demons are
    Ephememphi, associated with pleasure,
    Yoko, associated with desire,
    Nenentophni, associated with distress,
    Blaomen, associated with fear.
        Their mother is Esthesis-Zouch-Epi-Ptoe.[7]

Out from these four demons come passions:[8]
    From distress arise
        Envy, jealousy, grief, vexation, discord, cruelty,
          worry, mourning.
    From pleasure come much evil
        And unmerited pride,
        And so forth.
    From desire come
        Anger, fury, bitterness, outrage, dissatisfaction,
        And so forth.
    From fear emerge
        Horror, flattery, suffering, and shame.

[Their thought and truth is Anayo, the ruler of the
    material soul.
It belongs with the seven senses, Esthesis-Zouch-
    Epi-Ptoe.]

(continued on page 103)

9 The sequence of bodily parts, emotional functions, and so forth that we have seen in these last few sections of the Secret Book of John are evidently taken from a separate book entitled the Book of Zoroaster. Zoroaster, or Zarathushtra, founded the Persian religion that bore his name, Zoroastrianism; some Zoroastrian priests, the magi, appear in the story of Jesus's birth. It is a living religion, practiced by the Parsis of India. In the ancient world, Zoroastrian magi were renowned for their magical and astrological knowledge. It is not surprising to hear about a book of magical names credited to Zoroaster. The lists given here have not actually provided the names of all 365 demons, but we can be sure that other magical books did. There are good translations of magical texts from the Christian, Jewish, Greek, and Egyptian traditions, generally with all the traditions mixed together; magic recognized no boundaries (see Suggestions for Further Reading). This ancient medical literature was the religion of the people, quite far removed from the religion of the elite church fathers, and deserves more attention from scholars than it has received. In the Secret Book of John the practice of ancient magic-medicine receives a theoretical and cosmic foundation in Gnostic myth.

❖ Here the short version of the Secret Book of John resumes.

10 Despite all of their labors detailed in the previous pages, the demons' imitation of the image they saw reflected on the waters above them fails to live. It lies still, a corpse, in the condition of Genesis's Adam just after God has made him from clay and before any breath of life entered him.

11 Now Sophia, Yaldabaoth's mother, initiates the trap. To make Adam live and move, Yaldabaoth will lay the foundation for his own destruction by freeing the power that sustains him into Adam, who was created specifically for the purpose of receiving it and restoring it to its original place in the divine realms. Now Sophia does what she should have done before her fall, she asks assistance and permission from the Mother-Father.

This is the total number of the demons: 365.
They worked together to complete, part by part, the
    psychic and the material body.
There are even more of them in charge of other
    passions
        That I didn't tell you about.
        If you want to know about them
            You will find the information in the Book of
                Zoroaster.[9]

All of Yaldabaoth's servants and his demons
    Worked to finish the psychic body.
    For a very long time it lay inanimate;
    It did not move.[10]

Yaldabaoth's mother wanted to take back the power
    She had turned over to the chief ruler.
    She earnestly asked the most merciful,[11]
    The Mother-Father of everything,
        For help.

1 The Father-Mother, or Invisible Spirit, makes the next major move in this drama. The five lights—the Son-Autogenes-Christ, along with Harmozel, Oriel, Daveithai, and Eleleth—disguise themselves as the primary advisors of Yaldabaoth. These are, of course, not mythic people but representations of divine functioning. In the guise of Yaldabaoth's principal demons they are now implanting ideas that will lead to those demons' destruction through the removal of divine power.

2 To motivate Yaldabaoth to fall into the trap of giving the power to Adam, first the Image of Divine Humanity illuminated the waters above, next Yaldabaoth's demons brought a bodily representation of that Image into being, and now, to make that bodily representation live, the divine power will be blown into it. This is all a complex interpretation of the sequence of events told in Genesis 2:7, "The Lord God made man from the clay of the soil and blew the Spirit of Life into his nostrils in order that man might become a living being."

3 The plot is this: Adam, modeled on the higher divine world, will receive the divine power that empowers Yaldabaoth, his demons, and the lower world. Adam is the microcosm; the divine realms are the macrocosm. Once Adam has the power, Adam will be able to return that power to the realms of God by becoming fully aware of his origin and true nature and thus becoming able to ascend. The plot succeeds. The five lights persuade the ruler of the demons to risk his possession of divine power. That power leaves Yaldabaoth, enters Adam, and Adam lives and moves and illuminates the dark world below just as the Image that was projected on the waters above did.

□ Yaldabaoth Deceived

By his sacred command he sent down the five lights
    In the forms of the principal advisors to Yaldabaoth.
    [This led to the removal of Yaldabaoth's mother's
        divine power from him.][1]
They told Yaldabaoth:
    "Blow some of your Spirit in the man's face,
    Then his body will rise up."
Yaldabaoth blew some of his Spirit into the man.
    That Spirit was the divine power of his mother.[2]

[He didn't understand what was happening, for he lived
    in ignorance.]
His mother's divine power left Yaldabaoth
    It entered the psychic human body
    Modeled on the primordial image.

The human body moved!
    It grew powerful!
    It shone![3]

(continued on page 107)

4 | The demonic forces now come to realize that they have been tricked. Their creation outthinks them and they are threatened. One is reminded of the countless science fiction stories featuring robots who are vastly more intelligent than their creators and who threaten their creators. Adam is now intellectually superior to Yaldabaoth. The reference to his being "naked of evil" is an interpretation of Genesis 2:25: "The man and his wife were naked and were not ashamed."

5 | To thoroughly imprison Adam, he is expelled to the lowest depths, the realm ruled by Belias: the world of dark, cold material substance. In the previous pages Adam had existed in the demonic imitation aeons above this world as a psychic being who was not yet a hard, material, mortal man. That time is nearly over; now he enters the realm of matter. The mythology here is using physical and spatial metaphors for what remains a consistently psychological narrative; the fall into the material world is a fall into believing in the existence of an external, material world.

❖ | According to the Secret Book of John, human beings erroneously believe they are embedded in a material world when, in fact, they are spiritual beings and the material world is not really there at all. This world of matter is real only insofar as it is thought to be real; it was thought into being by Yaldabaoth and subsequently by human beings. With the help of creative insight (Epinoia) those erroneous thoughts will come to an end. Then the material world's provisional reality will come to an end. In the Gnostic Gospel of Truth it is written: "Since oblivion came into existence because the Father was not known, then if the Father comes to be known, oblivion will not exist from that moment on" (18:9). A synonymous syllogism occurs at 24:29: "Since the deficiency came into being because the Father was not known, therefore, when the Father is known, from that moment on the deficiency will no longer exist." Oblivion and deficiency are terms the Gospel of Truth uses for the material world and what the Secret Book of John calls the realm of Yaldabaoth. It really isn't there at all.

Yaldabaoth's demonic forces envied the man.
    Through their united efforts he had come into
      being
    They had given their power to him.
His understanding was far greater than that of those
    who had created him
    And greater than that of the chief ruler himself.

When they realized that he shone with light
    And could think better than they could
    And was naked of evil,[4]
They took him and cast him down
    Into the lowest depths of the material world.[5]

1 Our present view of the nature of human beings is that we are wholly integrated body-mind-soul-spirit beings. But the Secret Book of John values only the spiritual part of a human being; the remainder is basically only a dwelling place, even a prison, of the spirit. The Spirit, which is the power of the Divine that empowers the whole lower world, is to return to its home above, and God, the Mother-Father merciful one, will assist its homecoming.

2 God now sends a friend to Adam, a character in the myth who will play a complex and crucial role: the Epinoia of light, the woman of life. She is the worldly manifestation of God's compassion and Adam's helper; this is the way that the Secret Book of John understands Genesis 2:18 where God says he will make a partner for Adam.

3 Epinoia is a mental function, a psychological term. In English it can be rendered "reflection," "conceptualization," "intuition," or "to come to understanding through creative consciousness." Light-filled Epinoia appears in the Secret Book of John as a character, a personage, but like the other characters in the story, she is really a form of mental functioning, in this case the capacity to form correct conceptions of the Divine. A contextual definition of Epinoia would be "the capacity to understand one's divine origin and return to it."

4 Epinoia, as creative conceptualization, works within all human beings to help them recall their divine origins. In what might be the single most important sentence in the Secret Book of John, we read, *"She taught Adam about the way he could ascend, which is the way he had descended."* This is the principal point of the elaborate mythological production: if we can understand how it is that we humans came to exist in this world, apparently apart from God, we will be able to reverse the process, rise above this world, and merge again into God. The point of understanding this mythology is to gain a road map for the journey back, to reverse the process by understanding it.

□ The Beginning of Salvation

The blessed one,
    The Mother-Father
    The good merciful one
Looked compassionately upon the Mother's power
    Relinquished by the chief ruler.[1]

Since Yaldabaoth's demons might again overpower
    the perceptible psychic body
He sent down from his good Spirit a helper for Adam,[2]
    Out of his great compassion
A light-filled Epinoia emerged.[3]
    And he called her Life.

    She aids the entire creation
        Working with him
        Restoring him to the fullness.
    She taught Adam about the way his people had
      descended.
    She taught Adam about the way he could ascend,
        Which is the way he had descended.[4]

(continued on page 111)

109

5   The light-filled Epinoia is the creative consciousness within human beings mythologized as a personality. It is separate from the rulers and the passions they control. Through this capacity we can rise back to the world of the mind of God. This is the sort of thing Paul had in mind when he wrote, "We have the mind of Christ" (1 Corinthians 2:16).

❖   So far in this mythological story the human body has been psychic in nature, a body based on soul, more of an essence than a material reality, a house of demons more than a physical entity. Here, though, it becomes materially real. The more material anything is, from the point of view of the Secret Book of John, the more imprisoning and farther from God it is. Since the power of Sophia is now incorporated into Adam, and that power sustains all the demons of this underworld, they realize that imprisoning Adam and keeping him from exercising his divine capacity for insight is necessary for their very survival.

The light-filled Epinoia was hidden in Adam⁵
    So that the rulers wouldn't know about her
    For Epinoia would repair the disaster their mother
      had caused.

Adam was revealed because within him dwelt the
    shadow of light.
    His mental abilities were far greater than those of
      his creators.
        They had gazed upward and seen his exalted
          mental capability.

The host of rulers and demons plotted together
They mixed fire and earth and water
    Together with four blazing winds
    They melded them together in great turbulence.
Adam was brought into the shadow of death.

(continued on page 113)

6 Now that Adam is dressed up in a body, he is incorporated into a physiological tomb; Adam is no longer immortal. Note that the physical body is not a part of Adam's basic human nature, but an alien substance he would be better off without. There appear to be conceptual connections made between earth/matter, water/darkness, fire/desire, and wind/artificial spirit (following Howard Bream's interpretation—see Suggestions for Further Reading).

7 According to this brief summary comment by a scribe of the Secret Book of John, Adam is the first embodiment of the power that was separated from the higher realms; Epinoia will help restore that power through Adam's ability to understand how he descended and thus how he can ascend.

They intended to make him anew
> This time from
>> Earth,
>> Water,
>> Fire,
>> Wind,
> Which are
>> Matter,
>> Darkness,
>> Desire,
>> The Artificial Spirit.
> This all became a tomb,
> A new kind of body.
This all thieves bound the man in it,
> Enchained him in forgetfulness,
> Made him subject to dying.[6]

[His was the first descent
> And the first separation.
Yet the light-filled Epinoia within him will elevate his
> thinking.][7]

1 These passages, like others in the Secret Book of John, appear to combine somewhat different accounts. This is the revised story of Adam in the Garden of Eden. In Genesis 2:9, a "tree of life" is said to exist at the center of the garden, a tree that is delightful and good for food. The present account reverses that judgment, interpreting the tree as a tree of the life of demons and, accordingly, a dreadful creation.

2 We will hear more about the creation of an artificial spirit later in the Secret Book of John. The following sequence discusses the tree of knowledge, which is Epinoia, the true divine Spirit. As the two trees are contrasted in the myth, so the two spirits are contrasted in human life.

☐ Adam in Yaldabaoth's Paradise

The rulers took the man and put him into paradise
They told him to eat freely.

    [Their food is bitter; their beauty is corrupt.
    Their food is deceit; their trees are ungodliness.
    Their fruit is poison.
    Their promise is death.][1]

They placed the tree of their life into the middle of
    paradise.

    I will teach you (plural) the secret of their life,
    The plan that they made together about an artificial
        spirit.[2]

(continued on page 117)

3 The description of the dreadful "tree of their life" is one of the more poetic passages in the Secret Book of John. We heard earlier that Adam's material body is based on "dark ignorance and desire"; here, those qualities describe the tree, whose seed is desire. You could compare this thought to the teachings of Buddha, whose Noble Truths focus on the notion that desire is the seed of all human suffering.

4 We are now well into the Secret Book of John's revisions to the myth in Genesis or, as our author thought of it, correcting Moses's misunderstanding. The tree of knowledge really represents insight and proper conception of the realms above: the whole mind of God. Adam is reminded of those realms by the mental capacity Epinoia, who is symbolized by the tree. The demons, in order to keep the divine light in Adam available to them to sustain their world, order Adam not to use his Epinoia, his capacity for conceiving of God's pleroma, the fullness of God's realms.

5 Jesus, who sporadically appears in this text as its narrator, caused Adam to use his faculty of Epinoia. Or, as the story has it, Jesus caused Adam to eat from the tree of knowledge, taking the role of the serpent in Moses's version.

6 The serpent here takes on a new role: it brings about the consequences of eating from the tree, as set out in Genesis 3:16. According to Moses, childbearing and sexual desire are in accordance with God's orders, but here these things are forced upon people (represented by Adam) by Yaldabaoth (represented by the serpent). Exactly what the serpent caused people to eat is not mentioned, although presumably the serpent had them eat from the tree of their life described earlier.

Its root is bitter
Its branches are dead.
   Its shadow is hatred
   Its leaves are deception
The nectar of wickedness is in its blossoms.
   Its fruit is death
   Its seed is desire
It flowers in the darkness.
   Those who eat from it are denizens of Hades
   Darkness is their resting place.[3]

As for the tree called the Knowledge of Good and Evil
   It is the Epinoia of the light.
They commanded him not to eat from it,
Standing in front to conceal it,
   For fear that he might look upwards to the fullness
   And know the nakedness of his indecency.[4]

   [However, I caused them to eat.[5]
   I asked the Savior, "Lord, isn't it the serpent who
      caused Adam to eat?"
   He smiled and replied, "The serpent caused them to
      eat
   in order to produce the wickedness of the desire to
      reproduce
   that would make Adam helpful to him."][6]

(continued on page 119)

7 Now that Adam has the resources of the tree of knowledge, or Epinoia, to assist him in asserting himself against Yaldabaoth, and now that he has eaten from that tree (meaning he has exercised his creative conceptualization, which is what Epinoia is), Yaldabaoth counterattacks by making Adam forget everything he has just learned.

8 Jesus, the Savior, responds to John's question about this forgetfulness, saying that while it does occur in the true myth that the Secret Book of John is expounding, Moses misinterpreted the myth in his own book, Genesis. Moses wrote in 2:21 that God put Adam into a deep sleep so as to extract one of his ribs in order to make that rib into Eve. But, as the Secret Book of John understands the story, Yaldabaoth made Adam forget the knowledge granted him by the tree, or Epinoia, and that forgetfulness and lack of consciousness was Adam's sleep. As we will see, the Epinoia that is removed from him becomes Eve.

9 The prophet mentioned here is Isaiah, supposedly the prophet of Yaldabaoth. The passage Isaiah 6:10 is quoted here as evidence of Yaldabaoth's true intentions. It shows that Gnostics, like many others before and after them, could comb through the Bible to find prooftexts to support their own ideas.

The chief ruler, Yaldabaoth, knew that
    Because the light-filled Epinoia within Adam
    Made his mental abilities greater than his own,
    Adam had been disobedient.
In order to recover the power that he had put into
 Adam
    Yaldabaoth made Adam completely forgetful.[7]

    [I asked the Savior, "What is it to be 'completely
      forgetful'?"
    He replied, "It is not what Moses wrote in his first
      book:
    'He caused Adam to fall into deep sleep'
    Rather, Adam's perceptions were veiled
    And he became unconscious.[8]
    As he (Yaldabaoth) said through his prophet:
    "I will make their minds dull so that they do not see
      or understand."][9]

1 At this point, Adam has within him two divine elements. One is relatively inactive but supplies him, and the whole lower world, with light and life, what we have been calling the power. The other, Epinoia, is a mental capacity that has come into Adam thanks to the collective will of the fullness of God's mind, the pleroma. If Yaldabaoth has his way, it is a capacity that Adam will lose. While Yaldabaoth cannot take all the divine power from Adam, he does remove a portion of it.

2 Now, in a way similar to the process of the creation of Adam, Yaldabaoth constructs a female form after the model of Epinoia, which came down to Adam from the whole fullness of the mind of God. Yaldabaoth uses some of the divine power that is in Adam to make that female form. Adam was modeled upon the whole of the divine mind as displayed upon the upper water; Eve was modeled upon the divine Epinoia that came down to Adam from the whole divine mind.

3 The text again takes issue with Moses's interpretation of the foundational myth, declaring that Genesis 2:21–22 got it wrong. It was not Adam's rib, but Adam's divine power that served to create Eve. A Jewish interpretation of scripture is called midrash. Although the Secret Book of John reverses the polarity of Genesis, interpreting the actions of Genesis's God as the evil plots of Yaldabaoth and his demons, it nevertheless falls into the category of midrash. It assumes the existence of a true and correct myth but takes issue with Moses's particular exposition and retelling of that myth. The Secret Book of John is a far more accurate telling of the truth that lies behind Genesis, or so we are supposed to believe.

Woman Comes into Being

The light-filled Epinoia hid deep within Adam.
    The chief ruler tried to remove her from his ribcage
    But Epinoia cannot be captured.
Although the darkness pursued her it did not catch her.

The chief ruler did remove a portion of his power from
    Adam
        To create a person with a woman's form[1]
        Modeled on the light-filled Epinoia that had been
            manifested to him.
He placed the power removed from the man into the
    woman.[2]

[It did not happen the way Moses said it did:
"he took a rib and made the woman."][3]

(continued on page 123)

121

❖ | The myth at this point is a drama featuring Adam as a kind of playing field for the contest between the forces of darkness, led by Yaldabaoth, and the forces of light, primarily Epinoia. First the upper realm reveals an image of itself as perfect humanity. Yaldabaoth's forces make a psychic model of this, but it remains immobile. The five lights come to Yaldabaoth and talk him into breathing his divine power into Adam. Adam moves and is becoming able to have his light ascend, the process whereby Yaldabaoth would be destroyed. Next Epinoia arrives to enlighten Adam. So Yaldabaoth throws him down into a dark, material existence. The demons make a tree of "life," which really represents death, but a contrasting tree is revealed: the tree of knowledge, a symbol of Epinoia. Adam eats from it but then is knocked unconscious by Yaldabaoth who tries to remove Epinoia and divine power from Adam. Yaldabaoth is partly successful, but ends up with a female human being who also has light within and represents Epinoia and Life. She pulls Adam out of unconsciousness, dark drunkenness as it is called, and Adam recognizes her. Throughout all of this, Adam himself is passive, a stage on which a cosmic drama is enacted.

4 | The woman with Adam has a dual significance in this story. She is, on the one hand, the first female human being, Eve. But, on the other hand, she represents a mental capacity for conceptualization of the realm of God, Epinoia. Bear in mind that Epinoia is not a person but the Greek word for the human capacity for true insight and conceptualization.

Adam saw the woman standing next to him.
The light-filled Epinoia immediately appeared to
him
She raised up the veil that dulled his mind.
He sobered up from the dark drunkenness
And he recognized his own counterpart.[4]

(continued on page 125)

5 Adam should reunite with Epinoia for salvation. Eve represents Epinoia, and through salvific union, Adam's power can be restored above. Genesis is cited without direct correction for a change, although its meaning is now to be understood in a Gnostic manner. This quotation of Genesis 2:23–24 means, in this context, that Humanity (Adam) and Epinoia (Eve) should unite. In other words, people should use their divinely given capacity for creative conceptualization to realize their inherent divinity. We can see how a ritual of the bridal chamber could become important to Gnostics. Adam's union with his wife, Eve, represents the union of any human being with Epinoia, with remembrance of the world of divine fullness, the pleroma.

6 This section of the Secret Book of John seems to be a short independent poem. It is not really in accord with the rest of the document because usually the one who comes down is said to be Epinoia or, sometimes, Providence. Sophia, the last we heard of her, was moving despondently back and forth in the ninth sphere. Gnostics, however, were creative and not obsessed with rigid consistency as the orthodox were.

7 The image of an eagle upon the tree of knowledge is a splendid one. In this context "I" is Jesus, the narrator of the Secret Book of John. A scribe has added a comment that the tree is "Epinoia from the pure Providence," a notion that is in keeping with the overall pattern of ideas in the Secret Book of John. Epinoia (usually) and Providence, or Pronoia, (occasionally) are the words that describe the mental functions that remind human beings of their true divine Power and origin.

He said: "This is bone from my bones
     Flesh from my flesh."
Because of this a man will leave his mother and father
And be joined to a woman and those two will become
     one flesh.
          For they will send his helper to him.[5]

[Sophia, our sister, came down[6]
     Descending innocently
     So as to regain what she had lost.
Therefore she was called Life
     The Mother of the Living
     The One from the Providence of the Authority of
          Heaven.
By her assistance people can achieve perfect knowledge.]

I appeared as an eagle perched on the tree of knowledge,[7]
     [Which is the Epinoia from the pure Providence of
          Light]
In order to teach them
     And raise them up from sleep's depths.

(continued on page 127)

8 | A scribal comment brings us back to Genesis. It describes the condition of Adam and Eve as they were about to be expelled from Eden in the Genesis account; fallen and naked, they hide from God (3:7–10) or, as here, they move away from Yaldabaoth.

9 | Yaldabaoth's cursing his earth has to do with Genesis 3:17 where God says to Adam, "Cursed be the earth because of you." In Genesis 3:16, God says to Eve, "Your desire will be for your husband and he will be your master," a command that is understood here to be part of Yaldabaoth's strategy to imprison humanity.

10 | Yaldabaoth is again trying to capture and dominate the divine light/life/power (these appear to be used as synonyms) that sustains him to keep it from ascending back to its place of origin. Ironically, it is Adam and Eve's disobedience to the will of God that causes their expulsion from Paradise in the standard version of the story; here it is their obedience to the will of God (but disobedience to Yaldabaoth) that leads to their expulsion.

[For the two of them were fallen and aware of their
  nakedness.[8]
Epinoia appeared as a being full of light
She enlightened their minds.]

When Yaldabaoth discovered that they had moved
  away from him
  He cursed his earth.
  He located the woman as she was preparing herself
    for her man.
He gave the woman over so that the man might be her
  master
  Because he did not know the secret of the divine
    strategy.[9]

The man and woman were too terrified to renounce
  Yaldabaoth,
  Who showed his ignorance to his angels,
And he cast both of them out of paradise[10]
  Dressing them in heavy darkness.

The chief archon saw the young woman who was
  standing by Adam.
  He realized that the light-filled Epinoia of Life was
    within her.
  Yaldabaoth became completely ignorant.

(continued on page 129)

11 We have just heard that Adam believes he should dominate Eve sexually, now Yaldabaoth plots to do the same thing. But, to protect the light/life/power within Eve, the Providence of the higher realms removes it temporarily from her. The stress on the term *life* here relates to the statement in Genesis 3:20 that Eve was called "mother of the living."

12 The Secret Book of John envisions reality with a spiritual dimension, which is discussed as the full mind of God; a psychic dimension, which is ruled by a host of Yaldabaoth's named demons; and a material dimension, which is ruled by Yahweh and Elohim. The dichotomy of righteous Yahweh and unrighteous Elohim reminds one of the fact, revealed earlier, that Yaldabaoth's seven demonic authorities are each paired with a form of divine power.

13 Yaldabaoth rapes Eve and impregnates her, and two arch-demons are born. In the book of Genesis, and throughout the Hebrew Bible, the Jewish God is sometimes called Yahweh and sometimes called Elohim. Here it is assumed that these are two different demons, the product of forced intercourse between the greatest demon of this world and the shell of Eve, who is temporarily without divine power. The descriptions of Yahweh and Elohim are completely alien to Judaism, although they are mentioned here as part of the Secret Book of John's ongoing revisionist interpretation of Genesis, where both divine names often occur. The demons and authorities mentioned earlier in the text rule psychic space-time. These final two rule the material body and the world of matter.

[When the Providence of all saw what was going to
    happen
She sent assistants to remove divine life from Eve.][11]

Yaldabaoth raped Eve.
She bore two sons.

[Elohim was the name of the first.
Yahweh was the name of the second.
    Elohim has a bear's face.
    Yahweh has a cat's face.
        One is righteous;
        One is not.[12]
            Yahweh is righteous;
            Elohim is not.
Yahweh commands fire and wind.
Elohim commands water and earth.][13]

.

(continued on page 131)

14 Before the addition of the passages defining the offspring of Yald-abaoth as Yahweh and Elohim, the narrative probably defined Cain and Abel (Genesis 4:1–2) as demonic beings born from the rape of Eve. That notion fits well into the text's ongoing effort to critically recover the myth behind Moses's book, Genesis; later the text will declare that Seth is the real progenitor of the human race.

15 The rape of Eve accounts mythologically for the origin of sexual intercourse. The function of mythology in any culture is to tell the story of the origin of customs and facts; what happens in the myth happens forever. The ongoing process of sexual reproduction continually produces material bodies in which the divine power is trapped. Yaldabaoth fills those bodies with his artificial spirit: the forces of ignorance and passion that often dominate human thoughts.

16 The "two" here are Yahweh (Cain) and Elohim (Abel), the two subordinate arch-demons. The tomb they rule over is, in one sense, this entrapping world and, in another sense, the human body.

Yaldabaoth deceptively named the two: Cain and Abel.[14]

[From then until now sexual intercourse has persisted
   Thanks to the chief ruler
      Who put desire for reproduction into the woman
         who accompanies Adam.
Through intercourse the Ruler caused new human
   bodies to be produced
      And he blew his artificial spirit into each of them.][15]

Yaldabaoth installed the two with authority over
   natural elements
      So they can rule over the tomb.[16]

1 Now that sexual intercourse has been brought into being by Yaldabaoth, Adam and Eve practice it. Eve has evidently received divine power again; here she is Foreknowledge, which is used at this point as a synonym for Epinoia. The text is rarely clear as to when it is speaking of Eve as a symbol for such divine insight and when it is speaking of Eve as the primordial woman, but one should not expect myth to strive for clarity. The child Seth is now "the Son of Man." You will recall that at the outset of the story of humanity in the Secret Book of John, a voice from heaven said, "the Man exists *and* the Son of Man," causing the demonic powers to look to the waters above and see reflected there the image of the full mind of God, the pleroma. Adam was modeled on "the Man." Eve was modeled on the pleroma as it appeared in the light-filled Epinoia. Now Seth, born of those two, is modeled on "the Son of Man."

❖ Adam and Eve, given life by the divine power of Sophia, assisted by God's Epinoia, and using the technique of intercourse established by Yaldabaoth, now construct a child modeled on the Son of Man in the divine realms. This child is a mythological being establishing the primordial pattern for all human beings who will follow; they will be his offspring, the children of Seth. We too are children of Seth; we have already been modeled in the heavenly realm.

2 As the divine realms once projected the image of the divine man onto the waters above the heavens, so the divine image is now carried forward into Seth. The notion of Seth as the progenitor of the whole human race is so significant that many scholars today (like some of the ancient Christian heresy-hunters) call the Gnosticism of this text and others like it "Sethianism."

□ The Children of Seth Populate the World

Adam had intercourse with the image of his
  foreknowledge (prognosis).
He begot a son like the Son of Man
    And he called that son Seth
    Modeling him on the heavenly race in the higher
      realms.[1]

In the same way the mother sent down her Spirit,
    The image of herself
    A model of the full higher realm,
In order to prepare a place for the descent of the
  realms.[2]

(continued on page 135)

❖ | We were told earlier in the myth that the artificial spirit from Yaldabaoth is blown into each new human body; now we learn that the mother, Providence, also gives her Spirit to humanity. At various places in the text, that Spirit is called Epinoia, Prognosis, Pronoia (Providence), and Sophia (Wisdom); these words are not synonyms in Greek. The Secret Book of John is much more interested in the process whereby the divine self recalls its origin than in using consistent terminology. Whatever language is used, the point is that the full model of the divine realms is sent into Seth and by extension into all his descendants. The whole human race thus has a capacity of mind that will allow us to know our history and follow the path back to salvation. Yaldabaoth knows the higher realms only dimly and imperfectly; we can know them fully and return to our place there.

3 | Although humanity struggles to free itself from the material world through remembrance of the full mind of God above, Yaldabaoth repeatedly casts sleep, forgetfulness, or drunkenness upon them. The word *Gnostic* means "one who has knowledge," and that knowledge is the mythology related here. Knowledge lets us remember where we came from and become able to return there again, to learn the way we have come down so as to learn the way to ascend again. Forgetfulness is the demonic weapon that prevents this from happening. The waters of forgetfulness are in the river Lethe, a Greek mythic notion well known in the ancient world.

4 | The Secret Book of John, assembled as it is from a variety of texts and perspectives, is inconsistent in its theory of salvation. Sometimes enlightenment is said to be inherent in human beings through their faculty of creative conceptualization or through the divine power that dwells within them; sometimes enlightenment is said to be a Spirit from the heavens that descends into human beings who are prepared for enlightenment, but do not yet have it. Perhaps the two theories can be united through the idea that the faculty of creative conceptualization, Epinoia, prepares people to receive the fullness of the heavenly realms through the arrival of the Spirit.

The chief ruler, though, forced the humans to drink
From waters of forgetfulness[3]
So that they might not know their true place of
origin.

The children (of Seth) remained in this condition for a
while
In order that when the Spirit descends from the holy
realms[4]

(*continued on page 137*)

5 Here we have a simple statement of the soteriology, or theory of salvation, of the Secret Book of John. We, who are the children of Seth, remain forgetful, but the Holy Spirit will eventually descend to everyone in this life or in a life to come. We will all eventually be restored to the fullness, the pleroma, the whole and united mind of God from whence we came long ago. This is a suitable ending to the text. As it stands, however, it is only the first of several endings. Perhaps the text once ended here and then further additions were gradually made to it: a dialogue about the soul, a few more revisions of the Genesis story, and a poem about the triple descent of God's Providence.

The Spirit can raise up the children (of Seth) and heal
  them from all defects
And thus restore complete holiness to the fullness of
  God.[5]

1 John is the "I" in these passages and "Lord" or "Savior" is Jesus. At some point relatively early in the history of the Greek Secret Book of John this set of dialogues concerning the soul was added to the text, possibly at the same time as the additions at the beginning and the end of the text so as to present it as a revelation from Jesus to John. This section shares with that material a concern for the "immovable race." While the myth of the Secret Book of John focuses on the indwelling in human beings of cosmic light or power derived from Sophia, until now the text has taken no interest in the origin or fate of an individual person's soul. Here, though, the soul is the factor in need of salvation.

2 Until this point in the myth salvation has been presented as a form of remembrance, of creative conceptualization (using the faculty of Epinoia), or an understanding of the Divine through the assistance of Providence (Pronoia). Now, however, a moralistic tone enters the discussion. We are to avoid wickedness and do good and if we bear up under the stresses and troubles of this underworldly life we will eventually be rewarded with life eternal. This is more an orthodox Christian perspective than a Gnostic one.

Six Questions about the Soul

I asked the Savior, "Lord, will every soul be saved and enter the pure light?"[1]

He replied, "You are asking an important question, one that will be impossible to answer for anyone who is not a member of the unmoved race. They are the people upon whom the Spirit of Life will descend and the power will enable them to be saved and become perfect and be worthy of greatness. They expunge evil from themselves and they will care nothing for wickedness, wanting only that which is not corrupt. They will achieve freedom from rage, envy, jealousy, desire, or craving."

"The physical body will negatively affect them. They wear it as they look forward to the time when they will meet up with those who will remove it. Those people deserve indestructible eternal life. They endure everything, bearing up under anything that happens so that they can deserve the good and inherit life eternal."[2]

(continued on page 141)

3 | As in the previous dialogue, salvation here depends on the arrival of a "Spirit of Life," without which nobody can be saved. Indeed, as was the case with Adam, everyone requires the Spirit even to have the strength to stand. Through the arrival of the Spirit of Life, anyone can be transformed. However, waiting for the Holy Spirit to impart salvation is more of an orthodox or standard Christian idea than is seeking remembrance of our descent from divine realms into this earth. To achieve salvation through understanding how we came down from above and how we can return to that heavenly realm, and to do this by utilizing the faculty of creative insight, or Epinoia, is Gnostic. Passively awaiting the arrival of a Spirit of Life is less typically Gnostic.

4 | The idea of an artificial spirit counteracting the work of the Holy Spirit is not usually found in orthodox Christian writing. But even so, in 1 John in the New Testament we hear of a church community in crisis where some people claim to have the Spirit of Christ and declare that other people have a spirit of antichrist. The Apostle Paul regarded human flesh as inhabited by a spirit of sin that worked against the intentions of the Holy Spirit. So the idea of a person being an arena of two contending spirits was not unknown in ancient Christianity.

5 | The theory here is that human beings are a balance between an empowered soul and an artificial spirit. This is not far from Paul's vision of Christians as having within them both the Spirit of Christ and the spirit of sin and flesh leading them in opposite directions. People must depend on divine assistance to be saved from this situation, according to the Secret Book of John, and their behavior, their flight from wickedness, is a crucial factor. The word *power* in this passage does not seem to refer to the power that Sophia brought low—the power that sustains the world of Yaldabaoth and enlivens humanity—but rather it is a synonym for what previously was called the Spirit of Life.

Then I asked him, "Lord, what about the souls who didn't do these things even though the Spirit of Life's power descended on them?"[3]

He answered, "If the Spirit descends to people they will be transformed and saved. The power descends on everyone and, without it, no one can even stand up. After they are born, if the Spirit of Life increases in them, power comes to them and their souls are strengthened. Nothing then can lead them astray into wickedness. But if the artificial spirit comes into people, it leads them astray."[4]

Then I said, "Lord, when souls come out of the flesh where do they go?"

He replied, smiling, "If the soul is strong it has more of power than it has of the artificial spirit and so it flees from wickedness. With the assistance of the Incorruptible One that soul is saved and it attains eternal rest."[5]

I then asked him, "Lord, what of the souls of the people who do not know whose people they are? Where do they go?"

(continued on page 143)

6 Through the artificial spirit, as through Paul's spirit of sin and flesh, people are drawn toward wickedness. Forgetfulness, a primary weapon of Yaldabaoth against the human race from the beginning, is now characterized as a particular punishment and not, as before, as a component part of the human experience.

7 The "prison" here is not a place, but the human body. People cycle around and around from life to life through reincarnation. But the ultimate vision is very positive. Eventually all will be saved and, in good Gnostic fashion, they will be saved by knowledge that overcomes forgetfulness.

8 This is a pretty naïve question. It seems to imply that if people are going to be reincarnated they must be born through the usual sexual processes. Assuming this, how will their souls manage to shrink down and enter the reproductive organs of a father and a mother?

9 The answer is evasive and nearly incomprehensible. It seems to tell us that anyone who adheres to another person who has the Spirit of Life can be saved. If they are saved, then they will not have to enter any new body. That may be, but it does not seem to answer the question.

10 Like the author of 1 John in the New Testament, who is enraged at the "antichrists" who have left his church, the author of these dialogues is outraged at the thought that someone could have come to true knowledge (meaning, as in John's letter, that they have been members of the author's own group) only to turn away (leave that group entirely or join up with a different group).

He responded, "In those people the artificial spirit has grown strong and they have gone astray. Their souls are burdened, drawn to wickedness, and cast into forgetfulness."[6]

"When they come forth from the body, such a soul is given over to the powers created by the rulers, bound in chains, and cast into prison again. Around and around it goes until it manages to become free from forgetfulness through knowledge. And so, eventually, it becomes perfect and is saved."[7]

Then I asked, "Lord, how does the soul shrink down so as to be able to enter its mother or a man?[8]

He was happy that I asked this and said, "You are truly blessed because you have understood. The soul should be guided by another within whom is the Spirit of Life. It will be saved by that means and accordingly will not have to enter a body again.[9]

And I said, "Lord, what happens to the souls of people who achieved true knowledge, but who turned away from it?"[10]

(continued on page 145)

11   This passage is one of the very few in the Secret Book of John that is influenced by a specific New Testament passage. The idea of a blasphemer against the Spirit being eternally punished is found in Mark 3:28–30, but the idea of eternal punishment without the possibility of repentance contradicts the earlier assertion in this dialogue that all people will eventually become perfect and be saved.

12   The final question is a literary device marking a transition back to the mythological narrative.

He said to me, "Demons of poverty will take them to a place where there is no possibility of repentance. There they will stay until the time when those who blasphemed against the Spirit will be tortured and subjected to punishment forever."[11]

I asked, "Lord, where did the artificial spirit come from?"[12]

And he told me:

❖ After the intrusion of the dialogue of the six questions about the fate of the soul, we are back to mythology and the vocabulary we grew used to in the pages before the dialogue began. The dialogue had to do with the present and future, what will happen to souls now under various conditions. Mythology has to do with the primordial past when the events took place that structure reality forever.

1 The themes here are now familiar. The highest conceivable deity (beyond whom is the Inconceivable One) wishes to restore full harmony to the divine realms, the divine mind. To do this the deity provides the faculty of insight and conceptualization, Epinoia, that makes human beings superior to all demonic powers. Yaldabaoth is jealous of humans, but he fails to fully imprison them. These motifs have all been expressed previously in regard to Adam and Eve; here they are applied to the rest of humanity, "the children of the perfect race."

2 Yaldabaoth tries a new strategy here. To imprison humanity he creates fate: the arrangement of present and future that most people of the ancient world believed governed their lives. Through astrology and other occult systems, people tried to know and even manipulate their fate, but as a general rule everyone and everything was under the sway of fate. Even the gods, the angels, and the demons were subject to it. As the body imprisons the soul, fate imprisons the will. Since the power of Sophia is all the power that really exists in the lower world, anything that comes into being must come from that power. The myth crudely expresses this fact as the demons of Yaldabaoth mating with Sophia.

☐ Three Plots against Humanity

The Mother-Father is merciful,
 A Holy Spirit sympathizing with us.
Through the Epinoia of the Providence of the light
  It raises up the children of the perfect race
  Raising up their thought, their light eternal.

When the chief archon learned that they were elevated
 above him
  And that their mental ability surpassed his
He wanted to put a stop to their thought.
  But he did not know the extent of their mental
   superiority
And he could not stop them.[1]

He made a plan with his demons
 Who are his energies.
Each of them fornicated with Wisdom (Sophia)
  And produced fate,
  The last variety of imprisonment.[2]

(continued on page 149)

3 If there is a god of fate, Yaldabaoth is that god. We often think of fate as being either good or bad, sometimes pleasant and sometimes not, but here fate is a purely negative concept. It is an impersonal force for the crushing of human spirit; it is the bars on our prison. Yet, just a few paragraphs earlier we heard of the Epinoia brought to us by the benevolent Mother-Father above this world, bringing us the chance to escape fate forever.

4 The notion of fate as the imprisoning force of the world is from the common Greco-Roman way of thinking. But here we are brought back into the world of Jewish biblical thought as the Secret Book of John continues its revisionist work with Moses's book, Genesis. As usual, the divinity behind Genesis is not the benevolent God of Moses's Judaism but the evil ruler Yaldabaoth, who seeks to destroy humanity. He tries to do this through a flood of darkness, rather than through a flood of water.

Fate changes unpredictably
    It is of different sorts just as the demons are of
        different sorts.
Fate is hard.
Fate is stronger than
    The gods, the authorities, the demons, the
        generations of people
    Who are caught up in it.
Out of fate emerged
    Sinfulness, violence, blasphemy, forgetfulness,
        Ignorance,
            Weighty commandments
            Heavy sins
        Terrible fear.
In this way all of creation became blind,
    Ignorant of God above everything.

Because of imprisonment in forgetfulness
    They are unaware of their sins;
    They are bound into periods of time and seasons
By fate, who is lord of it all.[3]

Yaldabaoth eventually came to regret everything he
    had created.
    He decided to bring a great flood
    Upon creation, upon mankind.[4]

(continued on page 151)

<u>**5**</u>   Once more Moses is said to have gotten it wrong. The text here alludes to Genesis 7:7. We learn that the people of light, those who listen to Noah, hide in a cloud of light, thus saving themselves from the world-threatening powers of darkness. Yaldabaoth is foiled again. It is interesting to note that Yaldabaoth himself was hidden, at first, in a brilliant cloud of light.

<u>**6**</u>   This is a revision of passages in Genesis that tell the story of the sons of God. Unlike the story of Noah, the story of the sons of God mating with earthly women is rarely discussed in Christian churches and few people are even aware of it. Genesis 6:1–4 tells us that as people began to increase in numbers, more and more daughters were born. The sons of God found them beautiful and took as many wives from among them as they wished. After the sons of God had had intercourse with human women, sons were born. Then and subsequently Nephilim (giants), who were the renowned heroes of old, came down to the earth. Genesis 6:3 interjects the comment that God decided to remove the Spirit from human beings, to make them mortal. Immediately after this sequence of events, God decided to destroy the world through the flood, a lengthy account that begins with Genesis 6:5. All of this is the background for the ideas found in this section of the Secret Book of John. God's decision to remove the Spirit would be, from the usual Gnostic perspective, Yaldabaoth's effort to retrieve his mother's divine power. According to the Secret Book of John, the sons of God, who remain to this day a mysterious notion to Jewish and Christian theologians, are Yaldabaoth's demonic assistants sent to human women.

But the great light of Providence warned Noah.
>   He preached to all of the children,
>   The sons of men,
But if they were strangers to him they didn't listen.

>   [It was not the way Moses said: "they hid in an ark."
>   Rather, they hid in a special place,
>   Not just Noah but also many other people from the
>   immovable race.
>   They went into hiding within a cloud of light!][5]

Noah knew his own authority
>   And that of the Light Being who illuminated them,
>   Although the chief ruler poured darkness over all
>   the world.

The chief ruler and his powers plotted a strategy,
>   To send his demons to human daughters[6]
>   And make themselves children by them to enjoy.
But they failed.

After their failure they made another plan.
>   They created an artificial spirit
>   Modeled on the Spirit who descended
So, to impregnate souls by means of this spirit,
>   The demons changed appearance to look like the
>   women's husbands

(continued on page 153

7 | Women being filled with darkness and wickedness does not mean that men are free from this condition. Rather, the story is trying to account for the fact that the descendents of those women, which is to say the subsequent whole human race, are afflicted with a spirit of darkness and wickedness. Just as Yaldabaoth makes a world that is an artificial imprisoning version of the divine realms above, so he makes an artificial spirit to imprison people who can be freed by the Holy Spirit.

❖ | We have come to the end of the mythological history of God, the universe, and humanity as told in the Secret Book of John. Mythological time segues into the present time. The bleak Gnostic vision of most of humanity does seem to characterize the lives of many people. As Thomas Hobbes famously wrote in *The Leviathan* about the natural condition of humanity: "No arts, no letters, no society, and which is worst of all, continual fear and danger of violent death, and the life of man solitary, poor, nasty, brutish, and short."

8 | It rings true that "gold and silver, presents and money," and things of that sort were invented by demons to imprison people and keep them from focusing on higher things. It does often seem to work out that way.

9 | This final passage is a scribal summary of what has happened in the previous few pages. The whole of the Secret Book of John has quite a splendid sweep from the beginning before time down to "the present day." It does not end on this very gloomy note, however. Like a symphony whose last movement becomes slow and minor-key, but then finishes with a coda that brings it to a rousing, exciting, upbeat conclusion, so the Secret Book of John ends on a positive and affirmative poetic note, with a hymn to salvation brought to all the world three times through God's Providence.

They filled the women with that spirit of darkness
   and wickedness.[7]

They brought into being
   Gold and silver,
   Presents and money,
   Iron and other metals and all things of this sort.
And the people who were attracted were led astray into
   troubles
   And were greatly misled.
   And grew old
      Experiencing no pleasure
   And died
      Finding no truth
      Never knowing the true God.
This is the way that they enslaved all of creation
   From the foundation of the world until now.[8]

[They took some women and produced children out of
   darkness
   And they closed their hearts
   And they hardened themselves in the hardness of
      their artificial spirit
Until the present day.][9]

1 "Providence" is the English translation of the Greek psychological term *pronoia*. *Pro-noia* is "fore-thought," similar to *pro-gnosis* or "fore-knowledge." God's providence, in theology, means God's benevolent plan and intention for the whole universe. In the Secret Book of John, Providence is the saving knowledge that leads people to freedom from enclosure in this world. That saving knowledge has to do with what was announced in the prologue by Jesus, who is the "I" speaking throughout the Secret Book of John and who is the Christian-Gnostic Providence:

I have come to teach you
> About what is
> And what was
> And what will be
> In order for you to understand
>> The invisible world
>> And the world that is visible
>> And the immovable race of perfect humanity.

In other words, Providence is the whole of the Secret Book of John when it is properly understood. Providence teaches Adam about the way he can ascend, which is the way he had descended. So, Providence is not a person but rather a saving form of self-knowledge revealed by the Divine here in these pages. And yet, because the literature is mythological, Providence is depicted as a person.

❖ This hymn is not present in the short version of the Secret Book of John.

☐ The Providence Hymn

I am the Providence of everything.[1]
I became like my own human children.

I existed from the first.
I walked down every possible road.

I am the wealth of the light.
I am the remembering of the fullness.

I walked into the place of greatest darkness and on
    down.
I entered the central part of the prison.

The foundations of chaos quaked.

I hid because of their evil.
    They did not recognize me.

I came down a second time
    continuing on.

(continued on page 157)

2 Providence coming into the "middle of darkness," into the underworld, should be understood in at least two ways. The first way is most obvious: It is a mythological pattern of divine descent from the realms of light (discussed in detail at the beginning of the Secret Book of John) into the places of darkness (discussed at its end). The text traces the evolution of humanity from before the beginning of time until its final conclusion, which will be its reabsorption into the realms of light. The second way of understanding the passage is more difficult to conceive, because the realm of darkness and imprisonment for a human being is actually a material human body, the origins of which also have been dealt with in detail in these pages. The arrival of divine knowledge, Providence, into the body seems to be conceived here in reference to the effects of spirit possession, which usually causes the body to quake and even collapse. The entry into a human person by a divine person, which is spirit possession, is a violent and difficult experience, as attested in virtually all cultures including the Christian Pentecostal cultures. The arrival of Providence into a person is what this poem is really all about, not just its abstract mythological arrival into a lower world.

❖ The threefold Providence hymn probably originates in the wisdom tradition of ancient Judaism. There we find God's wisdom descending into the world, calling people to learn from her, speaking in the first person as an individual being. There we have poetry rather than mythology, because in official Jewish circles no one seriously thought of God as having subordinate aspects acting separately from him. Nevertheless, Wisdom is described in ancient Judaism much as Providence is in Gnosticism, and always with a completely positive connotation. In

(continued on page 158)

I emerged from among those of light
I am the remembering of Providence.

I entered the middle of darkness
   The inner part of the underworld[2]
   To pursue my mission.

The foundations of chaos quaked
   Threatening to collapse upon all who were there
   And utterly destroy them.

I soared upward again
   To my roots in light
   So as not to destroy them all yet.

I descended a third time.

I am light
I am dwelling in light
I am the remembering of Providence

I entered the midst of darkness
I came to the deepest part of the underworld.

I let my face light up
   Thinking of the end of their time
I entered their prison
   The body is that prison

(*continued on page 159*)

the Wisdom of Solomon 7:24–27, we read that "Wisdom is mobile above all motion, penetrating and pervading everything through her purity. She is a portion of the power of God, a pure essence of the Almighty's glory. Nothing impure enters within her. She reflects the eternal light, she is the mirror to God's power; she is the image of God's goodness. She can do everything; she renews herself and, in each generation, she comes into holy souls and makes them God's friends and his prophets." This sounds very much like Providence in the Secret Book of John.

❖ In Proverbs 1:22–23 it certainly sounds as if Wisdom were acting independently. She (for in Hebrew, as in Greek, the word for "wisdom" is feminine) speaks in direct address: "How long, you simpletons, will you love foolishness, how long will you reject my reproof? I will pour out my spirit to you and you will know my words." The idea here is that God's wisdom is available in the world, implicitly sent from God, to assist people in their ordinary and in their religious lives. In that context, Wisdom does not provide a form of religious salvation and she is not a savior.

❖ When the Gnostic tradition began to conceive of creation as a great cosmic mistake, and Jewish people of Gnostic orientation thought about the active power of creation in Proverbs as being the wisdom of God (Proverbs chapter 8), then Wisdom became the central figure in the crisis that brought about the world. At the same time, Gnostics sometimes seem to have thought of Wisdom as a savior, bringing human beings the spiritual power that would enable them to escape the world. The Secret Book of John, however, seems to vacillate between giving that role to divine Epinoia of light, which is human insight, and giving it to divine Pronoia, which is foresight or Providence. In terms of the history of these ideas, all such figures seem to trace back to the figure of Wisdom as is found in Proverbs, in the Wisdom of Solomon, and in other related books.

I cried out:
> "Anyone who hears,
> Rise up from your deep sleep!"

And the sleeping one awoke and wept
> Wiping bitter tears saying
>> "Who calls me?"
>> "Where has my hope come from
>> As I lie in the depths of this prison?"

"I am the Providence of pure light," I replied,
"I am the thought of the Virgin Spirit
> Raising you up to an honored place.
> Rise up!
Remember what you have heard.
> Trace back your roots
To me,
> The merciful one.
Guard against the poverty demons.
Guard against the chaos demons.
Guard against all who would bind you.
> Awaken!
> Stay awake!
> Rise out of the depths of the underworld!

(continued on page 161)

❖ This poem suitably draws the Secret Book of John to its conclusion. The whole story of the imprisonment of humanity ends with the arrival of salvation, the awakening of humanity, and humankind then arising out of prison back to light. Here the poem speaks directly to its audience, the readers and hearers of the Secret Book of John. You are taken out of the story of your primordial mythological past into your personal present.

3 This brief and enigmatic passage seems to presuppose religious ritual in the Gnostic community, a sealing or baptism of five seals. We know that Gnostic religion had ceremonies of baptism connected to the reception of true knowledge and this passage speaks of one such ritual.

❖ The concluding hymn was probably part of a ritual service. It would have been recited aloud by perfected members of the community who had won the right to identify themselves with saving knowledge. The purpose of Gnosticism is to enable human beings to ascend into the fullness of God, not just to tell tales of mythological beings ascending. One might imagine a Gnostic service with ascended members enacting the role of Providence and reciting the whole myth to new initiates.

I raised him up.
I sealed him with the light/water of the five seals,[3]
Death had no power over him ever again.

I ascend again to the perfect realm.
I completed everything and you have heard it."

1 Here the Secret Book of John concludes with a statement by Jesus Christ rather than by Providence, who was speaking earlier. The framing narrative about Jesus and John that began the work now ends it. This narrative serves to convert a document of Judeo-Platonic Gnosticism into Christian Gnosticism by changing the personage of the revealer from Providence, as in the previous poems, or Epinoia, who has that role throughout most of the mythological story, to Jesus Christ. For the Christian monks who may have read the book in their orthodox Pachomian monastery prior to 367 CE, when books such as these were ordered to be hidden or burned, Providence who came into the world to enlighten humanity was really Jesus, as were all forms of the forces of knowledge that continually struggled against Yaldabaoth.

2 The canonical book the Revelation to John also ends with warnings of this sort: "If anyone adds to the words in this book, God will add to him the plagues described in it. If anyone takes away words in this prophetic book, God will take away his share of the tree of life" (22:18–19).

☐ Conclusion

"I have told you everything now so that you can write
   it all down
And share it with your fellow spirits secretly,
For this is the mystery of the unmoved race."[1]

The Savior gave all of this to him to write and to keep
carefully. He said to him, "Anyone who exchanges it
for a present, or for food, or for drink, or for clothing,
or for anything else of that sort will be cursed."[2]

These things came to John in a mystery.
   Instantly the Savior vanished.
John came to his fellow disciples and told them what
   the Savior had said to him.

Jesus the Christ.
Amen.

The Apocryphon of John

Notes □

1. Irenaeus *Against Heresies* in *The Ante-Nicene Fathers,* ed. Rev. Alexander Roberts and James Donaldson (Buffalo: The Christian Literature Publishing Company, 1885), 2.4.2.
2. Ibid.
3. "Gospel of Truth," trans. George W. MacRae in *The Nag Hammadi Library in English,* rev. ed., ed. James Robinson (San Francisco: Harper & Row, 1988), 1.3.18:9–22, 24:28, 25:18.
4. "Gospel of Philip," trans. Wesley W. Isenberg in *The Nag Hammadi Library in English,* rev. ed., 1.2.3:61.
5. Irenaeus *Against Heresies,* 1.18.1.

Suggestions for Further Reading □

If you are interested in learning more about Gnostic texts, my home-page, http://home.epix.net/~miser17/Thomas.html, gives access not only to essays and translations of the Gospel of Thomas but is one of the Internet's richest sources of links to scholarly and popular sites on Gnosticism. The books listed below are available from this website.

Betz, Hans Dieter, ed. *The Greek Magical Papyri in Translation: Including the Demotic Spells.* 2nd ed. Chicago: University of Chicago Press, 1992. A stunning, fascinating, and comprehensive collection of magical spells used by the ordinary Christian, Jewish, and Pagan people of antiquity.

Bream, Howard N. *The Apocryphon of John and Other Coptic Translations.* Baltimore: Halgo Press, 1987. The only other commentary on the Secret Book of John written for the general reader. The author, a Christian seminary professor, takes a Christian view of the issues raised in the Secret Book of John but, nevertheless, his commentary is both positive and sympathetic.

Davies, Stevan, trans. and ann. *The Gospel of Thomas: Annotated and Explained.* Woodstock, Vt.: SkyLight Paths, 2002. The Gospel of Thomas is a new collection of Jesus's sayings. It is the most important historical source of information about Jesus apart from the New Testament Gospels. It was discovered at Nag Hammadi where it was the second text in Book II, preceded by the Secret Book of John.

King, Karen L. *What Is Gnosticism?* Cambridge, Mass.: Belknap Press, 2003. This book, by a professor at the Harvard University Divinity School, traces the rise of Gnosticism, discusses various forms it took, and shows how Gnosticism was treated by early Christians and how it has been treated by more recent scholars.

Layton, Bentley. *The Gnostic Scriptures: A New Translation with Annotations and Introductions.* Garden City, N.J.: Doubleday, 1987. Yale University professor Layton's footnotes to his translations are detailed and valuable for any student of these texts. He is one of America's leading Coptologists.

Meyer, Marvin, and Willis Barnstone, eds. *The Gnostic Bible.* Boston: Shambhala, 2003. This volume contains a whole host of different texts, some from Nag

Hammadi, some from the Manicheans, and some from other sources. These translations read more smoothly than some others do.

Meyer, Marvin, and Richard Smith, eds. *Ancient Christian Magic: Coptic Texts of Ritual Power.* San Francisco: HarperSanFrancisco, 1994. These translations are primarily from Coptic manuscripts and reveal a great deal about the life, belief, and rituals of ordinary Christian people, the people who read and used the Coptic Gnostic texts.

Pagels, Elaine. *The Gnostic Gospels.* New York: Random House, 1979. Pagels's book has been a best-seller, easily understood by nonprofessionals. It is not a survey of Gnosticism but a set of arguments on various interesting subjects by a well-respected Princeton University professor.

Robinson, James, ed. *The Nag Hammadi Library in English.* rev. ed. San Francisco: Harper & Row, 1988. This volume contains all of the books found at Nag Hammadi translated into English by a wide variety of respected scholars who have had the opportunity to revise and perfect their translations for this newer edition.

Rudolph, Kurt. *Gnosis: The Nature and History of Gnosticism.* San Francisco: Harper & Row, 1983. This is a survey of Gnosticism from its beginnings through its heyday in the second and third centuries and then into its decline. It is a complex book, but its careful organization will enable nonprofessionals to understand it.

Global Spiritual Perspectives

Spiritual Perspectives on America's Role as Superpower
by the Editors at SkyLight Paths

Are we the world's good neighbor or a global bully? Explores broader issues surrounding the use of American power around the world, including in Iraq and the Middle East. From a spiritual perspective, what are America's responsibilities as the only remaining superpower? Contributors:

Dr. Beatrice Bruteau • Rev. Dr. Joan Brown Campbell • Tony Campolo • Rev. Forrest Church • Lama Surya Das • Matthew Fox • Kabir Helminski • Thich Nhat Hanh • Eboo Patel • Abbot M. Basil Pennington, ocso • Dennis Prager • Rosemary Radford Ruether • Wayne Teasdale • Rev. William McD. Tully • Rabbi Arthur Waskow • John Wilson
5½ x 8½, 256 pp, Quality PB, ISBN 1-893361-81-0 **$16.95**

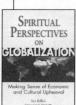

Spiritual Perspectives on Globalization, 2nd Edition
Making Sense of Economic and Cultural Upheaval
by Ira Rifkin; Foreword by Dr. David Little, Harvard Divinity School

What is globalization? What are spiritually minded people saying and doing about it? This lucid introduction surveys the religious landscape, explaining in clear and nonjudgmental language the beliefs that motivate spiritual leaders, activists, theologians, academics, and others involved on all sides of the issue. This edition includes a new Afterword and Discussion Guide designed for group use.
5½ x 8½, 256 pp, Quality PB, ISBN 1-59473-045-8 **$16.99**

Hinduism / Vedanta

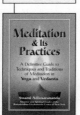

Meditation & Its Practices: A Definitive Guide to Techniques and Traditions of Meditation in Yoga and Vedanta
by Swami Adiswarananda

The complete sourcebook for exploring Hinduism's two most time-honored traditions of meditation. Drawing on both classic and contemporary sources, this comprehensive sourcebook outlines the scientific, psychological, and spiritual elements of Yoga and Vedanta meditation.
6 x 9, 504 pp, HC, ISBN 1-893361-83-7 **$34.95**

Sri Sarada Devi: Her Teachings and Conversations
Translated and with Notes by Swami Nikhilananda
Edited and with an Introduction by Swami Adiswarananda

Brings to life the Holy Mother's teachings on human affliction, self-control, and peace in ways both personal and profound, and illuminates her role as the power, scripture, joy, and guiding spirit of the Ramakrishna Order.
6 x 9, 288 pp, HC, ISBN 1-59473-070-9 **$29.99**

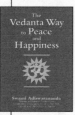

The Vedanta Way to Peace and Happiness
by Swami Adiswarananda

Using language that is accessible to people of all faiths and backgrounds, this book introduces the timeless teachings of Vedanta—divinity of the individual soul, unity of all existence, and oneness with the Divine—ancient wisdom as relevant to human happiness today as it was thousands of years ago.
6 x 9, 240 pp, HC, ISBN 1-59473-034-2 **$29.99**

Or phone, fax, mail or e-mail to: SKYLIGHT PATHS Publishing
Sunset Farm Offices, Route 4 • P.O. Box 237 • Woodstock, Vermont 05091
Tel: (802) 457-4000 • Fax: (802) 457-4004 • www.skylightpaths.com
Credit card orders: (800) 962-4544 (8:30AM–5:30PM ET Monday–Friday)
Generous discounts on quantity orders. SATISFACTION GUARANTEED. Prices subject to change.

Children's Spirituality

Because Nothing Looks Like God
by Lawrence and Karen Kushner; Full-color illus. by Dawn W. Majewski

Real-life examples of happiness and sadness—from goodnight stories, to the hope and fear felt the first time at bat, to the closing moments of life—introduce children to the possibilities of spiritual life.

11 x 8½, 32 pp, HC, Full-color illus., ISBN 1-58023-092-X **$16.95**

For ages 4 & up (a Jewish Lights book)

Also available:

Teacher's Guide, 8½ x 11, 22 pp, PB, ISBN 1-58023-140-3 **$6.95** *For ages 5–8*

Becoming Me: A Story of Creation
by Martin Boroson; Full-color illus. by Christopher Gilvan-Cartwright

Told in the personal "voice" of the Creator, here is a story about creation and relationship that is about each one of us.

8 x 10, 32 pp, Full-color illus., HC, ISBN 1-893361-11-X **$16.95** *For ages 4 & up*

But God Remembered: Stories of Women from Creation to the Promised Land   *by Sandy Eisenberg Sasso; Full-color illus. by Bethanne Andersen*

A fascinating collection of four different stories of women only briefly mentioned in biblical tradition and religious texts; all teach important values through their actions and faith.   9 x 12, 32 pp, HC, Full-color illus., ISBN 1-879045-43-5 **$16.95**

For ages 8 & up (a Jewish Lights book)

Cain & Abel: Finding the Fruits of Peace
by Sandy Eisenberg Sasso; Full-color illus. by Joani Keller Rothenberg

A sensitive recasting of the ancient tale shows we have the power to deal with anger in positive ways. Provides questions for kids and adults to explore together. "Editor's Choice"—American Library Association's *Booklist*

9 x 12, 32 pp, HC, Full-color illus., ISBN 1-58023-123-3 **$16.95** *For ages 5 & up (a Jewish Lights book)*

Does God Hear My Prayer?
by August Gold; Full-color photo illus. by Diane Hardy Waller

This colorful book introduces preschoolers as well as young readers to prayer and how prayer can help them express their own fears, wants, sadness, surprise, and joy.   10 x 8½, 32 pp, Quality PB, Full-color photo illus., ISBN 1-59473-102-0 **$8.99**

The 11th Commandment: Wisdom from Our Children
by The Children of America

"If there were an Eleventh Commandment, what would it be?" Children of many religious denominations across America answer this question—in their own drawings and words. "A rare book of spiritual celebration for all people, of all ages, for all time." —*Bookviews*

8 x 10, 48 pp, HC, Full-color illus., ISBN 1-879045-46-X **$16.95** *For ages 4 & up (a Jewish Lights book)*

For Heaven's Sake
by Sandy Eisenberg Sasso; Full-color illus. by Kathryn Kunz Finney

Everyone talked about heaven: "Thank heavens." "Heaven forbid." "For heaven's sake, Isaiah." But no one would say what heaven was or how to find it. So Isaiah decides to find out, by seeking answers from many different people.

9 x 12, 32 pp, HC, Full-color illus., ISBN 1-58023-054-7 **$16.95** *For ages 4 & up (a Jewish Lights book)*

God in Between
by Sandy Eisenberg Sasso; Full-color illus. by Sally Sweetland

If you wanted to find God, where would you look? A magical, mythical tale that teaches that God can be found where we are: within all of us and the relationships between us.   9 x 12, 32 pp, HC, Full-color illus., ISBN 1-879045-86-9 **$16.95**

For ages 4 & up (a Jewish Lights book)

Children's Spirituality

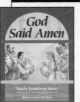

God Said Amen
by Sandy Eisenberg Sasso; Full-color illus. by Avi Katz

A warm and inspiring tale of two kingdoms that shows us that we need only reach out to each other to find the answers to our prayers.

9 x 12, 32 pp, HC, Full-color illus., ISBN 1-58023-080-6 **$16.95**
For ages 4 & up (a Jewish Lights book)

How Does God Listen?
by Kay Lindahl; Full-color photo illus. by Cynthia Maloney

How do we know when God is listening to us? Children will find the answers to these questions as they engage their senses while the story unfolds, learning how God listens in the wind, waves, clouds, hot chocolate, perfume, our tears and our laughter.

10 x 8½, 32 pp, Quality PB, Full-color photo illus., ISBN 1-59473-084-9 **$8.99**
For ages 3–6

In God's Name
by Sandy Eisenberg Sasso; Full-color illus. by Phoebe Stone

Like an ancient myth in its poetic text and vibrant illustrations, this award-winning modern fable about the search for God's name celebrates the diversity and, at the same time, the unity of all the people of the world.

9 x 12, 32 pp, HC, Full-color illus., ISBN 1-879045-26-5 **$16.95**
For ages 4 & up (a Jewish Lights book)

Also available in Spanish:

El nombre de Dios
9 x 12, 32 pp, HC, Full-color illus., ISBN 1-893361-63-2 **$16.95**

Where Does God Live?
by August Gold; Full-color photo illus. by Matthew J. Perlman

Using simple, everyday examples that children can relate to, this colorful book helps young readers develop a personal understanding of God.

10 x 8½, 32 pp, Quality PB, Full-color photo illus., ISBN 1-893361-39-X **$8.99**
For ages 3–6

In Our Image: God's First Creatures
by Nancy Sohn Swartz; Full-color illus. by Melanie Hall

A playful new twist on the Creation story—from the perspective of the animals. Celebrates the interconnectedness of nature and the harmony of all living things.   9 x 12, 32 pp, HC, Full-color illus., ISBN 1-879045-99-0 **$16.95**
For ages 4 & up (a Jewish Lights book)

Noah's Wife: The Story of Naamah
by Sandy Eisenberg Sasso; Full-color illus. by Bethanne Andersen

This new story, based on an ancient text, opens readers' religious imaginations to new ideas about the well-known story of the Flood. When God tells Noah to bring the animals of the world onto the ark, God also calls on Naamah, Noah's wife, to save each plant on Earth.

9 x 12, 32 pp, HC, Full-color illus., ISBN 1-58023-134-9 **$16.95**
For ages 4 & up (a Jewish Lights book)

Also available:

Naamah: Noah's Wife (A Board Book)
by Sandy Eisenberg Sasso, Full-color illus by Bethanne Andersen
5 x 5, 24 pp, Board Book, Full-color illus., ISBN 1-893361-56-X **$7.99** *For ages 0–4*

Children's Spirituality—Board Books

How Did the Animals Help God? (A Board Book)
by Nancy Sohn Swartz, Full-color illus. by Melanie Hall
Abridged from Nancy Sohn Swartz's *In Our Image*, God asks all of nature to offer gifts to humankind—with a promise that they will care for creation in return.
5 x 5, 24 pp, Board Book, Full-color illus., ISBN 1-59473-044-X **$7.99** *For ages 0–4*

Where Is God? (A Board Book)
by Lawrence and Karen Kushner; Full-color illus. by Dawn W. Majewski
A gentle way for young children to explore how God is with us every day, in every way. Abridged from *Because Nothing Looks Like God* by Lawrence and Karen Kushner.   5 x 5, 24 pp, Board, Full-color illus., ISBN 1-893361-17-9 **$7.95** *For ages 0–4*

What Does God Look Like? (A Board Book)
by Lawrence and Karen Kushner; Full-color illus. by Dawn W. Majewski
A simple way for young children to explore the ways that we "see" God. Abridged from *Because Nothing Looks Like God* by Lawrence and Karen Kushner.
5 x 5, 24 pp, Board, Full-color illus., ISBN 1-893361-23-3 **$7.95** *For ages 0–4*

How Does God Make Things Happen? (A Board Book)
by Lawrence and Karen Kushner; Full-color illus. by Dawn W. Majewski
A charming invitation for young children to explore how God makes things happen in our world. Abridged from *Because Nothing Looks Like God* by Lawrence and Karen Kushner.   5 x 5, 24 pp, Board, Full-color illus., ISBN 1-893361-24-1 **$7.95** *For ages 0–4*

What Is God's Name? (A Board Book)
by Sandy Eisenberg Sasso; Full-color illus. by Phoebe Stone
Everyone and everything in the world has a name. What is God's name? Abridged from the award-winning *In God's Name* by Sandy Eisenberg Sasso.
5 x 5, 24 pp, Board, Full-color illus., ISBN 1-893361-10-1 **$7.99** *For ages 0–4*

What You Will See Inside ...

This important new series of books is designed to show children ages 6–10 the Who, What, When, Where, Why and How of traditional houses of worship, liturgical celebrations, and rituals of different world faiths, empowering them to respect and understand their own religious traditions—and those of their friends and neighbors.

What You Will See Inside a Catholic Church
by Reverend Michael Keane; Foreword by Robert J. Keeley, Ed.D.
Full-color photographs by Aaron Pepis
A colorful, fun-to-read introduction to the traditions of Catholic worship and faith. Visually explains the common use of the altar, processional cross, baptismal font, votive candles, and more. 8½ x 10½, 32 pp, HC, ISBN 1-893361-54-3 **$17.95**
Also available in Spanish: **Lo que se puede ver dentro de una iglesia católica**
8½ x 10½, 32 pp, Full-color photos, HC, ISBN 1-893361-66-7 **$16.95**

What You Will See Inside a Mosque
by Aisha Karen Khan; Photographs by Aaron Pepis
Featuring full-page pictures and concise descriptions of what is happening, the objects used, the spiritual leaders and laypeople who have specific roles, and the spiritual intent of the believers. Demystifies the celebrations and ceremonies of Islam throughout the year.
8½ x 10½, 32 pp, Full-color photos, HC, ISBN 1-893361-60-8 **$16.95**

What You Will See Inside a Synagogue
by Rabbi Lawrence A Hoffman and Dr. Ron Wolfson; Full-color photos by Bill Aron
A colorful, fun-to-read introduction that explains the ways and whys of Jewish worship and religious life. Full-page photos; concise but informative descriptions of the objects used, the clergy and laypeople who have specific roles, and much more.
8½ x 10½, 32 pp, Full-color photos, HC, ISBN 1-59473-012-1 **$17.99**

Children's Spiritual Biography

Ten Amazing People
And How They Changed the World
by Maura D. Shaw; Foreword by Dr. Robert Coles
Full-color illus. by Stephen Marchesi

For ages 7 & up

Black Elk • Dorothy Day • Malcolm X • Mahatma Gandhi • Martin Luther King, Jr. • Mother Teresa • Janusz Korczak • Desmond Tutu • Thich Nhat Hanh • Albert Schweitzer

This vivid, inspirational, and authoritative book will open new possibilities for children by telling the stories of how ten of the past century's greatest leaders changed the world in important ways.

8½ x 11, 48 pp, HC, Full-color illus., ISBN 1-893361-47-0 **$17.95** *For ages 7 & up*

Spiritual Biographies for Young People—For ages 7 and up

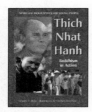
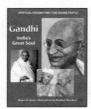

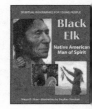

Black Elk: Native American Man of Spirit
by Maura D. Shaw; Full-color illus. by Stephen Marchesi
Through historically accurate illustrations and photos, inspiring age-appropriate activities, and Black Elk's own words, this colorful biography introduces children to a remarkable person who ensured that the traditions and beliefs of his people would not be forgotten.
6¾ x 8¾, 32 pp, HC, Full-color illus., ISBN 1-59473-043-1 **$12.99**

Dorothy Day: A Catholic Life of Action
by Maura D. Shaw; Full-color illus. by Stephen Marchesi
Introduces children to one of the most inspiring women of the twentieth century, a down-to-earth spiritual leader who saw the presence of God in every person she met. Includes practical activities, a timeline, and a list of important words to know.
6¾ x 8¾, 32 pp, HC, Full-color illus., ISBN 1-59473-011-3 **$12.99**

Gandhi: India's Great Soul
by Maura D. Shaw; Full-color illus. by Stephen Marchesi
There are a number of biographies of Gandhi written for young readers, but this is the only one that balances a simple text with illustrations, photographs, and activities that encourage children and adults to talk about how to make changes happen without violence. Introduces children to important concepts of freedom, equality, and justice among people of all backgrounds and religions.
6¾ x 8¾, 32 pp, HC, Full-color illus., ISBN 1-893361-91-8 **$12.95**

Thich Nhat Hanh: Buddhism in Action
by Maura D. Shaw; Full-color illus. by Stephen Marchesi
Warm illustrations, photos, age-appropriate activities, and Thich Nhat Hanh's own poems introduce a great man to children in a way they can understand and enjoy. Includes a list of important Buddhist words to know.
6¾ x 8¾, 32 pp, HC, Full-color illus., ISBN 1-893361-87-X **$12.95**

Kabbalah from Jewish Lights Publishing

Ehyeh: A Kabbalah for Tomorrow *by Dr. Arthur Green*
6 x 9, 224 pp, Quality PB, ISBN 1-58023-213-2 **$16.99**; HC, ISBN 1-58023-125-X **$21.95**

The Enneagram and Kabbalah: Reading Your Soul *by Rabbi Howard A. Addison*
6 x 9, 176 pp, Quality PB, ISBN 1-58023-001-6 **$15.95**

Finding Joy: A Practical Spiritual Guide to Happiness *by Dannel I. Schwartz with Mark Hass*
6 x 9, 192 pp, Quality PB, ISBN 1-58023-009-1 **$14.95**; HC, ISBN 1-879045-53-2 **$19.95**

The Gift of Kabbalah: Discovering the Secrets of Heaven, Renewing Your Life on Earth
by Tamar Frankiel, Ph.D.
6 x 9, 256 pp, Quality PB, ISBN 1-58023-141-1 **$16.95**; HC, ISBN 1-58023-108-X **$21.95**

Zohar: Annotated & Explained
Translation and annotation by Dr. Daniel C. Matt. Foreword by Andrew Harvey
5½ x 8½, 160 pp, Quality PB, ISBN 1-893361-51-9 **$15.99**

Meditation / Prayer

Prayers to an Evolutionary God
by William Cleary; Afterword by Diarmuid O'Murchu
How is it possible to pray when God is dislocated from heaven, dispersed all around us, and more of a creative force than an all-knowing father? Inspired by the spiritual and scientific teachings of Diarmuid O'Murchu and Teilhard de Chardin, Cleary reveals that religion and science can be combined to create an expanding view of the universe—an evolutionary faith.
6 x 9, 208 pp, HC, ISBN 1-59473-006-7 **$21.99**

The Song of Songs: A Spiritual Commentary
by M. Basil Pennington, OCSO; Illustrations by Phillip Ratner

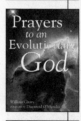

Join M. Basil Pennington as he ruminates on the Bible's most challenging mystical text. You will follow a path into the Songs that weaves through his inspired words and the evocative drawings of Jewish artist Phillip Ratner—a path that reveals your own humanity and leads to the deepest delight of your soul.
6 x 9, 160 pp, HC, 14 b/w illus., ISBN 1-59473-004-0 **$19.99**

Women of Color Pray: Voices of Strength, Faith, Healing, Hope, and Courage *Edited and with Introductions by Christal M. Jackson*
Through these prayers, poetry, lyrics, meditations and affirmations, you will share in the strong and undeniable connection women of color share with God. will challenge you to explore new ways of prayerful expression.
5 x 7¼, 240 pp, Quality PB, ISBN 1-59473-077-6 **$15.99**

The Art of Public Prayer, 2nd Edition: Not for Clergy Only
by Lawrence A. Hoffman 6 x 9, 288 pp, Quality PB, ISBN 1-893361-06-3 **$18.95**

Finding Grace at the Center: The Beginning of Centering Prayer
by M. Basil Pennington, OCSO, Thomas Keating, OCSO, and Thomas E. Clarke, SJ
5 x 7¼, 112 pp, HC, ISBN 1-893361-69-1 **$14.95**

A Heart of Stillness: A Complete Guide to Learning the Art of Meditation
by David A. Cooper 5½ x 8½, 272 pp, Quality PB, ISBN 1-893361-03-9 **$16.95**

Meditation without Gurus: A Guide to the Heart of Practice
by Clark Strand 5½ x 8½, 192 pp, Quality PB, ISBN 1-893361-93-4 **$16.95**

Praying with Our Hands: Twenty-One Practices of Embodied Prayer from the World's Spiritual Traditions *by Jon M. Sweeney; Photographs by Jennifer J. Wilson; Foreword by Mother Tessa Bielecki; Afterword by Taitetsu Unno, PhD*
8 x 8, 96 pp, 22 duotone photographs, Quality PB, ISBN 1-893361-16-0 **$16.95**

Silence, Simplicity & Solitude: A Complete Guide to Spiritual Retreat at Home
by David A. Cooper 5½ x 8½, 336 pp, Quality PB, ISBN 1-893361-04-7 **$16.95**

Three Gates to Meditation Practice: A Personal Journey into Sufism, Buddhism, and Judaism *by David A. Cooper* 5½ x 8½, 240 pp, Quality PB, ISBN 1-893361-22-5 **$16.95**

Women Pray: Voices through the Ages, from Many Faiths, Cultures, and Traditions
Edited and with introductions by Monica Furlong
5 x 7¼, 256 pp, Quality PB, ISBN 1-59473-071-7 **$15.99**;
Deluxe HC with ribbon marker, ISBN 1-893361-25-X **$19.95**

Midrash Fiction

Daughters of the Desert: Tales of Remarkable Women from Christian, Jewish, and Muslim Traditions   *by Claire Rudolf Murphy, Meghan Nuttall Sayres, Mary Cronk Farrell, Sarah Conover, and Betsy Wharton*

Breathes new life into the old tales of our female ancestors in faith. Uses traditional scriptural passages as starting points, then with vivid detail fills in historical context and place. Chapters reveal the voices of Sarah, Hagar, Huldah, Esther, Salome, Mary Magdalene, Lydia, Khadija, Fatima, and many more. Historical fiction ideal for readers of all ages.   5½ x 8½, 192 pp, HC, ISBN 1-893361-72-1 **$19.95**

The Triumph of Eve & Other Subversive Bible Tales
by Matt Biers-Ariel

Many people were taught and remember only a one-dimensional Bible. These engaging retellings are the antidote to this—they're witty, often hilarious, always profound, and invite you to grapple with questions and issues that are often hidden in the original text.   5½ x 8½, 192 pp, HC, ISBN 1-59473-040-7 **$19.99**

Religious Etiquette / Reference

How to Be a Perfect Stranger, 3rd Edition: The Essential Religious Etiquette Handbook   *Edited by Stuart M. Matlins and Arthur J. Magida*

The indispensable guidebook to help the well-meaning guest when visiting other people's religious ceremonies. A straightforward guide to the rituals and celebrations of the major religions and denominations in the United States and Canada, from the perspective of an interested guest of any other faith, based on information obtained from authorities of each religion. Belongs in every living room, library, and office. Covers:

African American Methodist Churches • Assemblies of God • Baha'i • Baptist • Buddhist • Christian Church (Disciples of Christ) • Christian Science (Church of Christ, Scientist) • Churches of Christ • Episcopalian and Anglican • Hindu • Islam • Jehovah's Witnesses • Jewish • Lutheran • Mennonite/Amish • Methodist • Mormon (Church of Jesus Christ of Latter-day Saints) • Native American/First Nations • Orthodox Churches • Pentecostal Church of God • Presbyterian • Quaker (Religious Society of Friends) • Reformed Church in America/Canada • Roman Catholic • Seventh-day Adventist • Sikh • Unitarian Universalist • United Church of Canada • United Church of Christ

6 x 9, 432 pp, Quality PB, ISBN 1-893361-67-5 **$19.95**

The Perfect Stranger's Guide to Funerals and Grieving Practices: A Guide to Etiquette in Other People's Religious Ceremonies   *Edited by Stuart M. Matlins*

6 x 9, 240 pp, Quality PB, ISBN 1-893361-20-9 **$16.95**

The Perfect Stranger's Guide to Wedding Ceremonies: A Guide to Etiquette in Other People's Religious Ceremonies   *Edited by Stuart M. Matlins*

6 x 9, 208 pp, Quality PB, ISBN 1-893361-19-5 **$16.95**

Spiritual Biography—SkyLight Lives

kyLight Lives reintroduces the lives and works of key spiritual figures of our time—people
/ho by their teaching or example have challenged our assumptions about spirituality and
ave caused us to look at it in new ways.

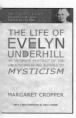   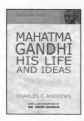

he Life of Evelyn Underhill
n Intimate Portrait of the Groundbreaking Author of *Mysticism*
y Margaret Cropper; Foreword by Dana Greene

velyn Underhill was a passionate writer and teacher who wrote elegantly on mysticism, wor-
iip, and devotional life. This is the story of how she made her way toward spiritual maturity,
om her early days of agnosticism to the years when her influence was felt throughout the world.
x 9, 288 pp, 5 b/w photos, Quality PB, ISBN 1-893361-70-5 **$18.95**

1ahatma Gandhi: His Life and Ideas
y Charles F. Andrews; Foreword by Dr. Arun Gandhi

xamines from a contemporary Christian activist's point of view the religious ideas and political
ynamics that influenced the birth of the peaceful resistance movement, the primary tool that
;andhi and the people of his homeland would use to gain India its freedom from British rule.
x 9, 336 pp, 5 b/w photos, Quality PB, ISBN 1-893361-89-6 **$18.95**

imone Weil: A Modern Pilgrimage
y Robert Coles

he extraordinary life of the spiritual philosopher who's been called both saint and mad-
oman. Robert Coles' intriguing study of Weil is an insightful portrait of the beloved and
ontroversial thinker whose life and writings influenced many (from T. S. Eliot to Adrienne
ich to Albert Camus), and continue to inspire seekers everywhere.
x 9, 208 pp, Quality PB, ISBN 1-893361-34-9 **$16.95**

en Effects: The Life of Alan Watts
y Monica Furlong

hrough his widely popular books and lectures, Alan Watts (1915–1973) did more to intro-
uce Eastern philosophy and religion to Western minds than any figure before or since. Here
the first and only full-length biography of one of the most charismatic spiritual leaders of
le twentieth century.
x 9, 264 pp, Quality PB, ISBN 1-893361-32-2 **$16.95**

More Spiritual Biography

ede Griffiths: An Introduction to His Interspiritual Thought
by Wayne Teasdale 6 x 9, 288 pp, Quality PB, ISBN 1-893361-77-2 **$18.95**

nspired Lives: Exploring the Role of Faith and Spirituality in the Lives of Extraordinary People
by Joanna Laufer and Kenneth S. Lewis 6 x 9, 256 pp, Quality PB, ISBN 1-893361-33-0 **$16.95**

piritual Innovators: Seventy-Five Extraordinary People Who Changed the World in
the Past Century *Edited by Ira Rifkin and the Editors at SkyLight Paths; Foreword by Robert Coles*
6 x 9, 304 pp, b/w photographs, Quality PB, ISBN 1-893361-50-0 **$16.95**; HC, ISBN 1-893361-43-8 **$24.95**

Vhite Fire: A Portrait of Women Spiritual Leaders in America
by Rabbi Malka Drucker; Photographs by Gay Block
7 x 10, 320 pp, 30+ b/w photos, HC, ISBN 1-893361-64-0 **$24.95**

Spirituality

Autumn: A Spiritual Biography of the Season
Edited by Gary Schmidt and Susan M. Felch; Illustrations by Mary Azarian
Autumn is a season of fruition and harvest, of thanksgiving and celebration o
abundance and goodness of the earth. But it is also a season that starkly an
realistically encourages us to see the limitations of our time. Warm and poignan
pieces by Wendell Berry, David James Duncan, Robert Frost, A. Bartle
Giamatti, Kimiko Hahn, P. D. James, Julian of Norwich, Garret Keizer, Trac
Kidder, Anne Lamott, May Sarton, and many others rejoice in autumn as a tim
of preparation and reflection.   6 x 9, 320 pp, 5 b/w illus., HC, ISBN 1-59473-005-9 **$22.9**

Awakening the Spirit, Inspiring the Soul
30 Stories of Interspiritual Discovery in the Community of Faiths
Edited by Brother Wayne Teasdale and Martha Howard, MD; Foreword by Joan Borysenka, Ph
Thirty original spiritual mini-biographies that showcase the varied ways tha
people come to faith—and what that means—in today's multi-religious worl
6 x 9, 224 pp, HC, ISBN 1-59473-039-3 **$21.99**

Winter: A Spiritual Biography of the Season
Edited by Gary Schmidt and Susan M. Felch; Illustrations by Barry Moser
Delves into the varied feelings that winter conjures in us, calling up both th
barrenness and the beauty of the natural world in wintertime. Includes sele
tions by Will Campbell, Rachel Carson, Annie Dillard, Donald Hall, Ro
Hansen, Jane Kenyon, Jamaica Kincaid, Barry Lopez, Kathleen Norris, Joh
Updike, E. B. White, and many others. "This outstanding anthology featur
top-flight nature and spirituality writers on the fierce, inexorable season of wi
ter.... Remarkably lively and warm, despite the icy subject." —*Publishe*
Weekly Starred Review

6 x 9, 288 pp, 6 b/w illus., Deluxe PB w/flaps, ISBN 1-893361-92-6 **$18.95**; HC, ISBN 1-893361-53-5 **$21.9**

The Alphabet of Paradise: An A–Z of Spirituality for Everyday Life
by Howard Cooper 5 x 7¾, 224 pp, Quality PB, ISBN 1-893361-80-2 **$16.95**

Creating a Spiritual Retirement: A Guide to the Unseen Possibilities in Our
Lives   *by Molly Srode*   6 x 9, 208 pp, b/w photos, Quality PB, ISBN 1-59473-050-42 **$14.99**;
HC, ISBN 1-893361-75-6 **$19.95**

The Geography of Faith: Underground Conversations on Religious, Political and
Social Change   *by Daniel Berrigan and Robert Coles; Updated introduction and afterword by
the authors*   6 x 9, 224 pp, Quality PB, ISBN 1-893361-40-3 **$16.95**

God Lives in Glass: Reflections of God for Adults through the Eyes of Children
by Robert J. Landy, PhD; Foreword by Sandy Eisenberg Sasso
7 x 6, 64 pp, HC, Full-color illus., ISBN 1-893361-30-6 **$12.95**

God Within: Our Spiritual Future—As Told by Today's New Adults
Edited by Jon M. Sweeney and the Editors at SkyLight Paths
6 x 9, 176 pp, Quality PB, ISBN 1-893361-15-2 **$14.95**

Jewish Spirituality: A Brief Introduction for Christians   *by Lawrence Kushner*
5½ x 8½, 112 pp, Quality PB, ISBN 1-58023-150-0 **$12.95** *(a Jewish Lights book)*

A Jewish Understanding of the New Testament
by Rabbi Samuel Sandmel; New preface by Rabbi David Sandmel
5½ x 8½, 384 pp, Quality PB, ISBN 1-59473-048-2 **$19.99**

Journeys of Simplicity: Traveling Light with Thomas Merton, Basho, Edward Abbey
Annie Dillard & Others   *by Philip Harnden* 5 x 7¼, 128 pp, HC, ISBN 1-893361-76-4 **$16.9**

Keeping Spiritual Balance As We Grow Older: More than 65 Creative Ways
to Use Purpose, Prayer, and the Power of Spirit to Build a Meaningful Retirement
by Molly and Bernie Srode 8 x 8, 224 pp, Quality PB, ISBN 1-59473-042-3 **$16.99**

The Monks of Mount Athos: A Western Monk's Extraordinary Spiritual Journey on
Eastern Holy Ground   *by M. Basil Pennington, ocso; Foreword by Archimandrite Dionysios*
6 x 9, 256 pp, 10+ b/w line drawings, Quality PB, ISBN 1-893361-78-0 **$18.95**

One God Clapping: The Spiritual Path of a Zen Rabbi   *by Alan Lew with Sherrill Jaffe*
5½ x 8½, 336 pp, Quality PB, ISBN 1-58023-115-2 **$16.95** *(a Jewish Lights book)*

Spirituality

Prayer for People Who Think Too Much
A Guide to Everyday, Anywhere Prayer from the World's Faith Traditions *by Mitch Finley*
5½ x 8½, 224 pp, Quality PB, ISBN 1-893361-21-7 **$16.95**; HC, ISBN 1-893361-00-4 **$21.95**

The Shaman's Quest: Journeys in an Ancient Spiritual Practice
by Nevill Drury; with a Basic Introduction to Shamanism by Tom Cowan
5½ x 8½, 208 pp, Quality PB, ISBN 1-893361-68-3 **$16.95**

Show Me Your Way: The Complete Guide to Exploring Interfaith Spiritual
Direction *by Howard A Addison* 5½ x 8½, 240 pp, Quality PB, ISBN 1-893361-41-1 **$16.95**;
HC, ISBN 1-893361-12-8 **$21.95**

Spirituality 101: The Indispensable Guide to Keeping—or Finding—Your Spiritual
Life on Campus *by Harriet L. Schwartz, with contributions from college students at nearly thirty
campuses across the United States* 6 x 9, 272 pp, Quality PB, ISBN 1-59473-000-8 **$16.99**

Spiritually Incorrect: Finding God in All the Wrong Places
by Dan Wakefield; Illus. by Marian DelVecchio
5½ x 8½, 192 pp, b/w illus., HC, ISBN 1-893361-88-8 **$21.95**

Spiritual Manifestos: Visions for Renewed Religious Life in America from Young
Spiritual Leaders of Many Faiths *Edited by Niles Elliot Goldstein; Preface by Martin E. Marty*
6 x 9, 256 pp, HC, ISBN 1-893361-09-8 **$21.95**

A Walk with Four Spiritual Guides: Krishna, Buddha, Jesus, and Ramakrishna
by Andrew Harvey 5½ x 8½, 192 pp, 10 b/w photos & illus., HC, ISBN 1-893361-73-X **$21.95**

What Matters: Spiritual Nourishment for Head and Heart
by Frederick Franck 5 x 7¼, 144 pp, 50+ b/w illus., HC, ISBN 1-59473-013-X **$16.99**

Who Is My God?, 2nd Edition
An Innovative Guide to Finding Your Spiritual Identity
Created by the Editors at SkyLight Paths 6 x 9, 160 pp, Quality PB, ISBN 1-59473-014-8 **$15.99**

Spirituality—A Week Inside

Come and Sit: A Week Inside Meditation Centers
Marcia Z. Nelson; Foreword by Wayne Teasdale
The insider's guide to meditation in a variety of different spiritual traditions.
Traveling through Buddhist, Hindu, Christian, Jewish, and Sufi traditions, this
essential guide takes you to different meditation centers to meet the teachers and
students and learn about the practices, demystifying the meditation experience.
6 x 9, 224 pp, b/w photographs, Quality PB, ISBN 1-893361-35-7 **$16.95**

Lighting the Lamp of Wisdom: A Week Inside a Yoga Ashram
John Ittner; Foreword by Dr. David Frawley
This insider's guide to Hindu spiritual life takes you into a typical week of retreat
inside a yoga ashram to demystify the experience and show you what to expect from
your own visit. Includes a discussion of worship services, meditation and yoga class-
es, chanting and music, work practice, and more. 6 x 9, 192 pp, b/w photographs, Quality
PB, ISBN 1-893361-52-7 **$15.95**; HC, ISBN 1-893361-37-3 **$24.95**

Making a Heart for God: A Week Inside a Catholic Monastery
Dianne Aprile; Foreword by Brother Patrick Hart
This essential guide to experiencing life in a Catholic monastery takes you to
the Abbey of Gethsemani—the Trappist monastery in Kentucky that was
home to author Thomas Merton—to explore the details. "More balanced and
informative than the popular *The Cloister Walk* by Kathleen Norris."
—*Choice: Current Reviews for Academic Libraries* 6 x 9, 224 pp, b/w photographs,
Quality PB, ISBN 1-893361-49-7 **$16.95**; HC, ISBN 1-893361-14-4 **$21.95**

Waking Up: A Week Inside a Zen Monastery
Jack Maguire; Foreword by John Daido Loori, Roshi
An essential guide to what it's like to spend a week inside a Zen Buddhist
monastery. 6 x 9, 224 pp, b/w photographs, Quality PB, ISBN 1-893361-55-1 **$16.95**;
HC, ISBN 1-893361-13-6 **$21.95**

Spiritual Practice

Divining the Body
Reclaim the Holiness of Your Physical Self by Jan Phillips
A practical and inspiring guidebook for connecting the body and soul in spiritual practice. Leads you into a milieu of reverence, mystery, and delight helping you discover a redeemed sense of self.
8 x 8, 256 pp, Quality PB, ISBN 1-59473-080-6 **$16.99**

Finding Time for the Timeless
Spirituality in the Workweek by John McQuiston II
Simple, refreshing stories that provide you with examples of how you can refocus and enrich your daily life using prayer or meditation, ritual, and other forms of spiritual practice. 5½ x 6½, 208 pp, HC, ISBN 1-59473-035-0 **$17.99**

The Gospel of Thomas: A Guidebook for Spiritual Practice
by Ron Miller; Translations by Stevan Davies
An innovative guide to bring a new spiritual classic into daily life. Offers a way to translate the wisdom of the Gospel of Thomas into daily practice, manifesting in your life the same consciousness revealed in Jesus of Nazareth. Written for readers of all religious backgrounds, this guidebook will help you to apply Jesus's wisdom to your own life and to the world around you.
6 x 9, 160 pp, Quality PB, ISBN 1-59473-047-4 **$14.99**

The Knitting Way: A Guide to Spiritual Self-Discovery
by Linda Skolnik and Janice MacDaniels
Through sharing stories, hands-on explorations, and daily cultivation, Skolnik and MacDaniels help you see beyond the surface of a simple craft in order to discover ways in which nuances of knitting can apply to the larger scheme of life and spirituality. Includes original knitting patterns.
7 x 9, 192 pp, Quality PB, ISBN 1-59473-079-2 **$16.99**

Earth, Water, Fire, and Air: Essential Ways of Connecting to Spirit
by Cait Johnson 6 x 9, 224 pp, HC, ISBN 1-893361-65-9 **$19.95**

Forty Days to Begin a Spiritual Life
Today's Most Inspiring Teachers Help You on Your Way
Edited by Maura Shaw and the Editors at SkyLight Paths; Foreword by Dan Wakefield
7 x 9, 144 pp, Quality PB, ISBN 1-893361-48-9 **$16.95**

Labyrinths from the Outside In
Walking to Spiritual Insight—A Beginner's Guide
by Donna Schaper and Carole Ann Camp
6 x 9, 208 pp, b/w illus. and photographs, Quality PB, ISBN 1-893361-18-7 **$16.95**

Practicing the Sacred Art of Listening: A Guide to Enrich Your
Relationships and Kindle Your Spiritual Life—The Listening Center Workshop
by Kay Lindahl 8 x 8, 176 pp, Quality PB, ISBN 1-893361-85-3 **$16.95**

The Sacred Art of Bowing: Preparing to Practice
by Andi Young 5½ x 8½, 128 pp, b/w illus., Quality PB, ISBN 1-893361-82-9 **$14.95**

The Sacred Art of Chant: Preparing to Practice
by Ana Hernandez 5½ x 8½, 192 pp, Quality PB, ISBN 1-59473-036-9 **$15.99**

The Sacred Art of Fasting: Preparing to Practice
by Thomas Ryan, CSP 5½ x 8½, 176 pp, Quality PB, ISBN 1-59473-078-4 **$15.99**

The Sacred Art of Listening: Forty Reflections for Cultivating a Spiritual
Practice *by Kay Lindahl; Illustrations by Amy Schnapper*
8 x 8, 160 pp, Illus., Quality PB, ISBN 1-893361-44-6 **$16.99**

Sacred Speech: A Practical Guide for Keeping Spirit in Your Speech
by Rev. Donna Schaper 6 x 9, 176 pp, Quality PB, ISBN 1-59473-068-7 **$15.99**;
HC, ISBN 1-893361-74-8 **$21.95**

Spiritual Poetry—The Mystic Poets

Experience these mystic poets as you never have before. Each beautiful, compact book includes: A brief introduction to the poet's time and place; a summary of the major themes of the poet's mysticism and religious tradition; essential selections from the poet's most important works; and an appreciative preface by a contemporary spiritual writer.

   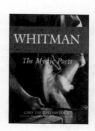

Hafiz: The Mystic Poets
Preface by Ibrahim Gamard
Hafiz is known throughout the world as Persia's greatest poet, with sales of his poems in Iran today only surpassed by those of the Qur'an itself. His probing and joyful verse speaks to people from all backgrounds who long to taste and feel divine love and experience harmony with all living things.
5 x 7¼, 144 pp, HC, ISBN 1-59473-009-1 **$16.99**

Hopkins: The Mystic Poets
Preface by Rev. Thomas Ryan, CSP
Gerard Manley Hopkins, Christian mystical poet, is beloved for his use of fresh language and startling metaphors to describe the world around him. Although his verse is lovely, beneath the surface lies a searching soul, wrestling with and yearning for God.
5 x 7¼, 112 pp, HC, ISBN 1-59473-010-5 **$16.99**

Tagore: The Mystic Poets
Preface by Swami Adiswarananda
Rabindranath Tagore is often considered the "Shakespeare" of modern India. A great mystic, Tagore was the teacher of W. B. Yeats and Robert Frost, the close friend of Albert Einstein and Mahatma Gandhi, and the winner of the Nobel Prize for Literature. This beautiful sampling of Tagore's two most important works, *The Gardener* and *Gitanjali,* offers a glimpse into his spiritual vision that has inspired people around the world.
5 x 7¼, 144 pp, HC, ISBN 1-59473-008-3 **$16.99**

Whitman: The Mystic Poets
Preface by Gary David Comstock
Walt Whitman was the most innovative and influential poet of the nineteenth century. This beautiful sampling of Whitman's most important poetry from *Leaves of Grass,* and selections from his prose writings, offers a glimpse into the spiritual side of his most radical themes—love for country, love for others, and love of Self.
5 x 7¼, 192 pp, HC, ISBN 1-59473-041-5 **$16.99**

Sacred Texts—SkyLight Illuminations Series
Andrew Harvey, series editor

Offers today's spiritual seeker an enjoyable entry into the great classic texts of the world's spiritual traditions. Each classic is presented in an accessible translation, with facing pages of guided commentary from experts, giving you the keys you need to understand the history, context, and meaning of the text. This series enables readers of all backgrounds to experience and understand classic spiritual texts directly, and to make them a part of their lives. Andrew Harvey writes the foreword to each volume, an insightful, personal introduction to each classic.

Bhagavad Gita
Annotated & Explained
Translation by Shri Purohit Swami; Annotation by Kendra Crossen Burroughs
"The very best Gita for first-time readers." —Ken Wilber. Millions of people turn daily to India's most beloved holy book, whose universal appeal has made it popular with non-Hindus and Hindus alike. This edition introduces you to the characters, explains references and philosophical terms, shares the interpretations of famous spiritual leaders and scholars, and more.
5½ x 8½, 192 pp, Quality PB, ISBN 1-893361-28-4 **$16.95**

Dhammapada
Annotated & Explained
Translation by Max Müller and revised by Jack Maguire; Annotation by Jack Maguire
The Dhammapada—believed to have been spoken by the Buddha himself over 2,500 years ago—contain most of Buddhism's central teachings. This timeless text concisely and inspirationally portrays the route a person travels as he or she advances toward enlightenment and describes the fundamental role of mental conditioning in making us who we are.
5½ x 8½, 160 pp, b/w photographs, Quality PB, ISBN 1-893361-42-X **$14.95**

The Gospel of Thomas
Annotated & Explained
Translation and annotation by Stevan Davies
Discovered in 1945, this collection of aphoristic sayings sheds new light on the origins of Christianity and the intriguing figure of Jesus, portraying the Kingdom of God as a present fact about the world, rather than a future promise or future threat.
5½ x 8½, 192 pp, Quality PB, ISBN 1-893361-45-4 **$16.95**

Hasidic Tales
Annotated & Explained
Translation and annotation by Rabbi Rami Shapiro
Introduces the legendary tales of the impassioned Hasidic rabbis, which demonstrate the spiritual power of unabashed joy, offer lessons for leading a holy life, and remind us that the Divine can be found in the everyday.
5½ x 8½, 240 pp, Quality PB, ISBN 1-893361-86-1 **$16.95**

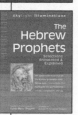

The Hebrew Prophets
Selections Annotated & Explained
Translation and annotation by Rabbi Rami Shapiro
Focuses on the central themes covered by all the Hebrew prophets: moving from ignorance to wisdom, injustice to justice, cruelty to compassion, and despair to joy, and challenges us to engage in justice, kindness, and humility in every aspect of our lives.
5½ x 8½, 224 pp, Quality PB, ISBN 1-59473-037-7 **$16.99**

Sacred Texts—SkyLight Illuminations Series
Andrew Harvey, series editor

The Hidden Gospel of Matthew: Annotated & Explained
Translation and annotation by Ron Miller
Takes you deep into the text cherished around the world to discover the words and events that have the strongest connection to the historical Jesus. Reveals the underlying story of Matthew, a story that transcends the traditional theme of an atoning death and focuses instead on Jesus's radical call for personal transformation and social change.
5½ x 8½, 272 pp, Quality PB, ISBN 1-59473-038-5 **$16.99**

The Secret Book of John
The Gnostic Gospels—Annotated & Explained
Translation and annotation by Stevan Davies

Introduces the most significant and influential text of the ancient Gnostic religion. This central myth of Gnosticism tells the story of how God fell from perfect Oneness to imprisonment in the material world, and how by knowing our divine nature and our divine origins—that we are one with God—we reverse God's descent and find our salvation.
5½ x 8½, 208 pp, Quality PB, ISBN 1-59473-082-2 **$16.99**

Rumi and Islam: Selections from His Stories, Poems, and
Discourses—Annotated & Explained
Translation and annotation by Ibrahim Gamard

Offers a new way of thinking about Rumi's poetry. Focuses on Rumi's place within the Sufi tradition of Islam, providing insight into the mystical side of the religion—one that has love of God at its core and sublime wisdom teachings as its pathways.
5½ x 8½, 240 pp, Quality PB, ISBN 1-59473-002-4 **$15.99**

Selections from the Gospel of Sri Ramakrishna
Annotated & Explained
Translation by Swami Nikhilananda; Annotation by Kendra Crossen Burroughs

The words of India's greatest example of God-consciousness and mystical ecstasy in recent history. Introduces the fascinating world of the Indian mystic and the universal appeal of his message that has inspired millions of devotees for more than a century.
5½ x 8½, 240 pp, b/w photographs, Quality PB, ISBN 1-893361-46-2 **$16.95**

The Way of a Pilgrim: Annotated & Explained
Translation and annotation by Gleb Pokrovsky

This classic of Russian spirituality is the delightful account of one man who sets out to learn the prayer of the heart—also known as the "Jesus prayer"—and how the practice transforms his life.
5½ x 8½, 160 pp, Illus., Quality PB, ISBN 1-893361-31-4 **$14.95**

Zohar: Annotated & Explained
Translation and annotation by Daniel C. Matt

The best-selling author of *The Essential Kabbalah* brings together in one place the most important teachings of the Zohar, the canonical text of Jewish mystical tradition. Guides you step by step through the midrash, mystical fantasy, and Hebrew scripture that make up the Zohar, explaining the inner meanings in facing-page commentary.
5½ x 8½, 176 pp, Quality PB, ISBN 1-893361-51-9 **$15.99**

About SKYLIGHT PATHS Publishing

SkyLight Paths Publishing is creating a place where people of differer spiritual traditions come together for challenge and inspiration, a plac where we can help each other understand the mystery that lies at the hea of our existence.

Through spirituality, our religious beliefs are increasingly becoming a part c our lives—rather than *apart* from our lives. While many of us may be mor interested than ever in spiritual growth, we may be less firmly planted in tra ditional religion. Yet, we do want to deepen our relationship to the sacred, t learn from our own as well as from other faith traditions, and to practice i new ways.

SkyLight Paths sees both believers and seekers as a community that increa ingly transcends traditional boundaries of religion and denomination—peo ple wanting to learn from each other, *walking together, finding the way.*

For your information and convenience, at the back of this book we have provided a list of other SkyLight Paths books you might find interesting and useful. They cover the following subjects:

Buddhism / Zen	Gnosticism	Mysticism
Catholicism	Hinduism /	Poetry
Children's Books	Vedanta	Prayer
Christianity	Inspiration	Religious Etiquette
Comparative	Islam / Sufism	Retirement
Religion	Judaism / Kabbalah /	Spiritual Biography
Current Events	Enneagram	Spiritual Direction
Earth-Based	Meditation	Spirituality
Spirituality	Midrash Fiction	Women's Interest
Global Spiritual	Monasticism	Worship
Perspectives		

Or phone, fax, mail or e-mail to: SKYLIGHT PATHS Publishing
Sunset Farm Offices, Route 4 • P.O. Box 237 • Woodstock, Vermont 05091
Tel: (802) 457-4000 • Fax: (802) 457-4004 • www.skylightpaths.com
Credit card orders: (800) 962-4544 (8:30AM–5:30PM ET Monday–Friday)
Generous discounts on quantity orders. SATISFACTION GUARANTEED. Prices subject to change.